NIGHTSPEEDER

The Black Coat Script Library

forthcoming

NIGHTSPEEDER

screenplay by
Emma Bull & Will Shetterly

illustrations by
Kevin O'Neill

A Black Coat Press Book

Acknowledgements: We are indebted to Stephan Martiniere, Kevin O'Neill for the use of his illustrations and David McDonnell for proofreading the typescript.

Visit our website at www.blackcoatpress.com

Finn
(*alternate designs*)

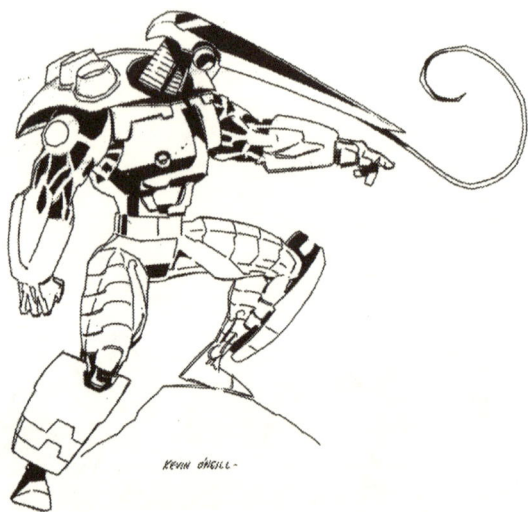

Introduction

There was a time, not so long ago, when you had to go to Japan if you wanted to see a really exciting animated science fiction film.

Anime features such as Hayao Miyazaki's *Nausicaa*, Katsuhiro Otomo's *Akira* and Masamune Shirow's *Ghost in the Shell* were on the cutting edge of science fiction, both in terms of story content as well as graphics. One of the theories we heard was that this type of material was being produced for animation in Japan simply because it could not be made in live action.

In the West, there was *Heavy Metal*, and that had been made nearly 20 years before. In our career with French artist Moebius (co-founder of the magazine *Heavy Metal*), we had tried to produce another similarly cutting edge animated science fiction epic, based on his graphic novel *The Airtight Garage*. The most cogent feedback we ever received from a studio executive (other than wanting to get rid of the hero's pith helmet) was, "But will it play in Peoria?" (We kid you not.)

We will never know, of course, if *The Airtight Garage* would have "played in Peoria," but since then, innovative features such as *The Matrix* trilogy, *Dark City* and *Star Wars: Attack of the Clones*, have proved that special effects technology has advanced to a sufficient degree to no longer be restricted to animation when it comes to producing vast, ambitious science fiction dramas. In fact, as the son pays homage to the father, *The Animatrix* returned to the source from which it had sprung and commissioned Japanese *anime* directors to produce their own visions within its fantastic universe.

In 1997, in between these two "ages," *Nightspeeder* was created, in the ever-ambitious desire to make a Western *anime* feature to rival those produced in Japan.

To create a properly eye-popping, never-seen-before visual environment for the original concept, the producers (the undersigned) called on British artist Kevin O'Neill, world-famous today for his stunning work on *The League of Extraordinary Gentlemen*. Kevin was provided with a basic concept, no more than an idea really, which eventually became an eight-page wordless comic story entitled *Nightspeeder*, published for the first (and only) time in the late, lamented French science fiction magazine *Kog*, in its second issue dated November 2001.

To take this pit of a concept and create a juicy, tasty fruit around it required exceptional writers. We were fortunate at the time to read a terrific script entitled *War for the Oaks* (also available in the Black Coat Script Library) by Emma Bull and Will Shetterly, adapting Emma's own novel.

Because the plan was for *Nighspeeder* to be made on a modest budget, Emma and Will had to work under certain limitations, such as adhering to a shorter running time, using a more limited cast and, of course, leaving plenty of room for the story to be carried by Kevin's visuals. So if you think the last sequence seems a little flat, play director. Think of your favorite science fiction battles and be assured that this would have been even better.

And who knows? It still *might*... While the interest in making adult animation in this country has never been lower, the fantastic progress of CG graphics have now opened new vistas for live action films. Perhaps *Nightspeeder* in all its glory will one day be coming to a theater near you.

Jean-Marc & Randy Lofficier

Nightspeeder
by Kevin O'Neill

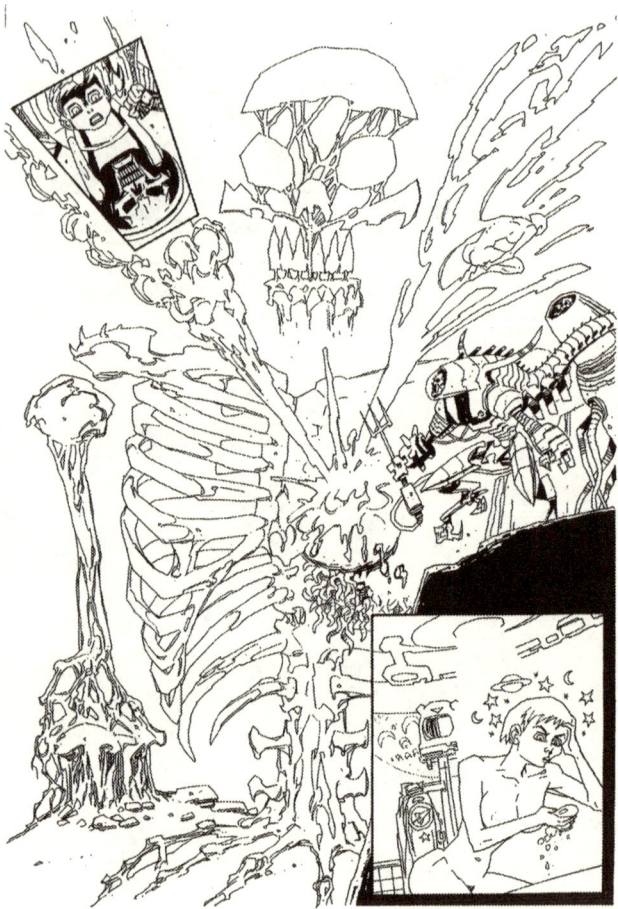

Nightspeeder

FADE IN:

<u>EXT. QUITO, ECUADOR - DAY</u>
Quito at the end of the twenty-first century is a glistening jewel set in a clear blue sky. With its green parks and glass towers, it appears to be paradise on Earth.

SUPERIMPOSE: *QUITO, ECUADOR, 2092 A.D.*

The skyscrapers reach toward Heaven, but one structure touches it. The STARBRIDGE, a slender tower reaching into space, is an elevator system that connects the Earth to an orbiting space station.

SUPERIMPOSE: *SITE OF STARBRIDGE 2.*

Flying cars and scooters whiz through the city. Below are pedestrian malls, greenways, commuter stations and parks. The buildings are laced together with public transportation: four-passenger capsules on monorails, and sliding pedestrian walkways running through clear tubes high above the ground.

<u>INT. CITY SLIDEWAYS - DAY</u>
FINN, an attractive young woman with short red hair, strides along the slideway toward the Starbridge. She wears the uniform of a starship pilot, simple, practical and close-fitting. She carries a small shoulder bag.

Her fellow COMMUTERS wear bright, strange clothes. Some are dressed in kimonos, dashikis, suits. Others wear clothes that change color or move like living things. They are Latinos, Asian, African, Caucasian: every nation has representatives here.

A slideway RIDER, seeing FINN's uniform, points and whispers excitedly to his companions. ANOTHER RIDER smiles and nods at her. FINN smiles back.

Three TEENAGERS, two boys and a girl, dart through the crowd, kicking and passing a small, vigorously rebounding ball.

A middle-aged BUSINESSMAN with a backpack finds himself in the middle of the game and scolds furiously. The teenagers race past FINN, and she laughs.

FINN steps off the slidewalk at "Starbridge Station."

INT. STARBRIDGE LOBBY - DAY
FINN crosses a bustling lobby where TRAVELERS carry briefcases, backpacks and suitcases that float in the air.

Security GUARDS stand before a row of huge elevator doors, checking tickets of travelers bound for the Starbridge.

FINN walks past the line of people waiting to board the elevators. A GUARD waves her past his checkpoint.

                    GUARD
        Morning, Nightspeeder. Have a safe jump.

                    FINN
        That's the plan. Thanks.

INT. STARBRIDGE ELEVATOR - DAY
FINN boards a windowed elevator capsule with rows of seats. Nineteen people board with her: young FAMILIES, COUPLES and a MAN and a WOMAN in technician's overalls.

Quito rapidly dwindles below them. A few people read. Most gawk, clearly making their first trip up the Starbridge.

A FATHER (an Asian man), a MOTHER (a brown-skinned woman) and TADAO, their 14-year-old son, sit near FINN.

KAZ spots FINN, and his eyes widen.

> KAZ
> Hey! You're a Nightspeeder!

His parents look away from the windows.

> FATHER
> Kaz. Your manners.

> KAZ
> (to Finn)
> My name's Kaz. I'm going to be a Nightspeeder, too.

> FINN
> It's a good job.

> FATHER
> But a dangerous one.

> FINN
> Not really. We've only lost one ship in six years.

> KAZ
> The *Cairo*, carrying one thousand passengers.

> FINN
> You've been doing your research.

KAZ nods, grinning.

> MOTHER
> You should see his room. Full of books and disks and posters about ships and probe pilots.

FINN
It's tough to qualify. Better bust your butt at school.

KAZ
What's hyperspace really like?

FINN
(grinning)
Want me to show you?

KAZ
You can do that?

FINN pulls what looks like sunglasses with attached headphones out of her bag. There's a dial on one earpiece.

MOTHER
What's that?

FINN
The simulator pilots use before a flight. To make sure
we haven't lost our edge.

KAZ
(putting on the goggles)
Zow!

EXT. HYPERSPACE SIMULATION
KAZ is floating in something like an infinite space of televi-
sion static.

FINN (V.O.)
Imagine something. A bird.

KAZ
OK.

20

KAZ concentrates. A cartoon bird takes shape before him.

                    KAZ
        All right!

The bird disintegrates back into the static.

                    KAZ
        I had it!

                    FINN (V.O.)
        You learn to maintain the concentration that keeps it
        there. Now, imagine a tunnel through the stuff around
        you.

A long tunnel forms, parting the static.

INT. STARBRIDGE ELEVATOR - DAY
                    FINN
        Got it?

                    KAZ
        Yeah. This is all there is to being a Nightspeeder?

                    FINN
        Yep. You manipulate hyperspace with your mind.
        But you're in beginner mode now. This is the
        standard test setting.

FINN cranks up the dial over KAZ's ear.

EXT. HYPERSPACE SIMULATION
The static-like environment begins to churn madly.

                    KAZ
        Whoa!

KAZ's tunnel swirls out of control. Vaguely human shapes form within it. KAZ spins wildly, buffeted by the chaos.

INT. STARBRIDGE ELEVATOR - DAY
FINN lifts the glasses off KAZ's head and puts them back in her bag. KAZ gasps, dazed and relieved.

> FINN
> That's why Nightspeeder training takes five years.

> KAZ
> Gotcha.

His mother and father smile at each other.

> MOTHER
> We're going to Deneb Three. Where're you heading?

> FINN
> I'm your pilot.

> KAZ
> Nightspeeder Finn? From the *Brazilia*? It's the biggest!

> FINN
> She's the queen of hyperspace. Four thousand passengers.

> FATHER
> Are you ever afraid?

> FINN
> Of what?

FATHER

Of going mad. I thought that's why passengers travel
in suspended animation.

FINN

I've made sixty-three flights, no problems. Don't
worry, I'll take care of you.

Starbridge Station looms above them. The elevator slows; its
occupants feel the effects of weightlessness.

EXT. STARBRIDGE STATION

Starbridge Station consists of four enormous metal rings connected to the tower like wheels on an axle. The lower three
rings spin to provide artificial gravity.

The fourth, furthest and largest ring doesn't rotate. Eighteen
ships connect to it by long, flexible tubes large enough for
people and cargo to pass through. Three ships are huge hyperspace transports.

The *Brazilia* is the largest and newest of all. It's beautiful, but
not aerodynamic–it looks a piece of jewelry or sculpture made
of polished silver.

INT. STARBRIDGE ELEVATOR

At Level Three, the doors open to reveal a uniformed STEW-
ARD.

STEWARD

Welcome to Starbridge Two! Hyperspace passengers,
this is your stop. Suspended animation services are to
your left at the end of the corridor.

Everyone but FINN and the technicians leaves the elevator,
moving awkwardly without gravity. KAZ turns to FINN.

                              KAZ
Bye, Nightspeeder.

                              FINN
Bye, Kaz. I hope you like life on Deneb Three.

                            FATHER
It's nice knowing we're in good hands.

INT. STARBRIDGE STATION - ELEVATOR STOP
FINN and the technicians float out of the elevator near a sign
reading, "LEVEL 4." FINN grabs a moving cable set into the
wall. It pulls her through the tube to the outer ring.

INT. STARBRIDGE STATION - OUTER RING
FINN arrives at the junction of several corridors. They're busy
with people doing their jobs. FLIGHT PERSONNEL and
small vehicles maneuver gracefully in weightlessness.

EDUARDO VEGA, a dark, handsome young man in a flight
controller's uniform, appears around the curve of the hallway,
riding the moving cable on the other side of the hall. He has a
bag hanging, holster-style, from his belt.

                          EDUARDO
        Finn!

FINN smiles. EDUARDO lets go of the cable, pushes off from
the wall and floats across the corridor. He grabs the cable beside her. They hug awkwardly, one-handed.

                              FINN
        Eduardo. You didn't have to see me off. We'll talk
        before the jump.

                          EDUARDO
        Sure. But I wanted to tell you–

                               24

He shrugs, then takes a red rose out of his bag and offers it to her. She looks at it, but doesn't reach for it.

FINN
The last two weeks were a lot of fun. But it's time to move on.

EDUARDO
Moving on doesn't mean you can't come back.

FINN
It's simpler if we don't expect anything.

EDUARDO
What's simplest isn't always what's best. Matters of the heart are never simple.

FINN
Co-workers shouldn't get involved.

EDUARDO
Why not?

FINN
It's awkward when it doesn't work out.

EDUARDO
Everything's awkward when it doesn't work out.

FINN
I've got to go.

EDUARDO
I know. Please. Take it.
                    (offering the rose, smiling)
It's the fastest way to get rid of me.

FINN
(embarrassed)
I don't want to get rid–

EDUARDO
And it'll let you take a tiny piece of Earth with you.

FINN
Well.
(accepting the rose)
We'll talk at preflight.

EDUARDO
About that. We're showing fluctuations in the ion
levels at the hyperspace gates.

FINN
They always fluctuate.

EDUARDO
Not like this. You may have to scrap the run.

FINN
What, and lose my bonus for a perfect flight record?

EDUARDO
You shouldn't joke–

FINN
See? You're too serious. We'd never work out.

EDUARDO
You've got the passengers to think of.

FINN
Most of them are boxed already, right?

EDUARDO

Yes, but–

FINN

If I scrub the flight, they get unpacked and have to
hang around for thirty days' recovery. And the
company loses hundreds of millions–

EDUARDO

They'll lose a lot more if something happens to the
Brazilia.

FINN

If it was really dangerous, the decision wouldn't be
the pilot's.

EDUARDO

We lost the *Cairo*–

FINN

Under conditions a lot worse than this. Don't worry,
Eduardo. I happen to be pretty good at what I do.

EDUARDO

You are, aren't you?

She kisses him on the cheek. EDUARDO lets go of the cable
and clutches at his heart with both hands. Drifting away, he
smiles as though struck dumb with love.

FINN laughs. EDUARDO grabs the cable on the opposite
wall. As it whisks him out of sight, he waves. FINN waves
back.

At an intersection, FINN releases the cable. A chute in the
nearby wall is labelled "TRASH" in eight languages.

She lifts the rose as if to drop it in the trash. Then she looks at the rose, shrugs, kicks off the wall and floats down the smaller corridor with the rose still in her hand.

INT. STARBRIDGE STATION - SMALLER CORRIDOR
FINN snags a handhold at the *Brazilia*'s air lock. She waves at WORKERS preparing for her ship's departure.

FINN
All secure?

WORKER
Just a few stand-by passengers to load.

FINN passes through the air lock into the ship.

INT. *BRAZILIA* CARGO BAY
Four thousand colonists sleep in transparent capsules. FINN studies them as she drifts past. They are men, women and children of all ages and races.

A CARGO LOADER enters the ship. She drives a floating vehicle loaded with 16 people in suspended animation capsules.

CARGO LOADER
These are the last, Nightspeeder.

FINN
Thanks.

FINN watches as the last colonists are secured in the cargo bay. They include KAZ and his family.

INT. *BRAZILIA* COCKPIT - EARTH ORBIT
FINN settles into the Nightspeeder's padded chair in the cockpit.

Before her is a vast viewscreen, showing the outside of her ship, the hold full of colonists' capsules, Earth floating in space and transmissions from the Flight Controller.

From a small refrigerator, FINN takes a bulb of water with a built-in straw. She shoves the rose stem down the straw, then presses the bulb against a wall. It sticks there.

>   FINN
>   Load navigator, Lizzardo interface, reference
>   Finn-421-B.

LIZZARDO appears, sitting on the edge of the control console. He's an 18-inch-tall hologram of a cartoon dinosaur.

>   LIZZARDO
>   On-line.

>   FINN
>   How's the ship?

>   LIZZARDO
>   All systems go.

>   FINN
>   You're talking like an antique again.

>   LIZZARDO
>   They had style in pre-space days. Know what a
>   shim-sham-shimmy is?

>   FINN
>   Not only do I not want to know, I'm afraid to ask
>   where you found it.

>   LIZZARDO
>   It's a dance.

A line of little LIZZARDOS and BELLY-DANCERS appear over the console and dance the shim-sham-shimmy to a swing tune.

FINN laughs, then shakes her head.

> FINN
> It's time for pre-flight.

All the dancers except LIZZARDO disappear.

> FINN
> Guidance linkage up.

FINN is linked to the guidance system by streams of light directed at receptors on her neck, temples and wrists.

> LIZZARDO
> I thought you seemed a little down.

> FINN
> I'm fine. What do the med and psych sensors say?

> LIZZARDO
> That you're a little down.

> FINN
> So you took some initiative? I'm not sure artificial intelligence is such a great idea.

> LIZZARDO
> (smugly)
> Yes, you are.

FINN taps the part of the viewscreen devoted to Flight Control. EDUARDO's face appears. Behind him, TECHNICIANS hover over racks of instruments.

FINN

Nightspeeder Finn of the *Brazilia* requesting final
data and clearance.

EDUARDO

Finn, we're reading level two anomalies in the
hyperspace environment.

FINN

Any sign of increasing activity?

EDUARDO

None.

FINN

Any problem with the Deneb beacon?

EDUARDO

It's at full signal strength.

FINN

Then I'm go for departure?

EDUARDO hesitates, as if he'd like to argue.

EDUARDO

You are.

FINN

Thank you. Initiating launch.

EXT. *BRAZILIA* - SPACE
The ship accelerates gracefully away from the Starbridge.

INT. *BRAZILIA* COCKPIT
FINN checks displays and moves her fingers through floating
holograms of colored light.

As she works, musical notes sound and colors flash and change.

>   FINN
>   Ship systems?

>   LIZZARDO
>   A-OK.

>   FINN
>   Passengers?

>   LIZZARDO
>   All stable.

>   FINN
> Flight Control, preparing to translocate.

>   EDUARDO
>   Clear for translocation.

FINN makes a dramatic pass over the ship's controls.

EXT. *BRAZILIA* - SPACE
The Brazilia slows. A dozen small robots leave the surface of the ship and form an enormous circle ahead of it.

INT. *BRAZILIA* COCKPIT
FINN watches the robots on the viewscreen. She moves her hands in an intricate pattern through the control holograms.

>   FINN
>   Configuring jump gate.

EXT. *BRAZILIA* - SPACE
The robots spin in place, then emit beams of red light, linking them in an enormous spiderweb of light.

INT. *BRAZILIA* COCKPIT
FINN makes a single decisive movement among the controls.

                    FINN
        Opening gate.

EXT. *BRAZILIA* - SPACE
In the space between the robots, a rift opens before the ship: a crack in space full of the surreal, kaleidoscopic craziness of hyperspace. Real hyperspace is far weirder than the simulation KAZ saw.

INT. *BRAZILIA* COCKPIT
FINN nods with satisfaction.

                    LIZZARDO
        The gate's open and stable.

                    FINN
        The Deneb beacon?

                    LIZZARDO
        Initiating contact... There!

EXT. *BRAZILIA* - SPACE
A beam of bright yellow light leaps from the center of the open gate and touches a sensor on the ship's surface.

INT. *BRAZILIA* COCKPIT
                    LIZZARDO
        Beacon signal at ninety-nine percent.

                    FINN
        Fine.

FINN taps the Flight Control panel on the viewscreen.

                              FINN
             We have the beacon. We're ready to jump.

EDUARDO appears on FINN's viewscreen.

                            EDUARDO
             Ion fluctuations are up. Readings are peaking twenty
             percent higher than an hour ago. The last spike was
             sixteen-point-seven.

                              FINN
             What's the time between peaks?

                            EDUARDO
             They're not regular.

                              FINN
             Eduardo, the beacon signal strength's at ninety-nine
             percent.

                           LIZZARDO
             Ninety-eight.

                              FINN
             Ninety-eight percent. If we go now, with a strong
             signal, we'll be in and out before the storm develops.

                            EDUARDO
             It's your decision, but–

                              FINN
             I say, "Let's go."

                            EDUARDO
             Good luck, then, Finn.

FINN
You, too, Eduardo. *Brazilia* out.

The image from Flight Control winks off the viewscreen.

LIZZARDO
"Not regular" is an understatement. These levels are jumping like a flea with a thyroid problem.

FINN
And what you're trying to say is...

LIZZARDO
(suddenly formal)
As navigator, I recommend waiting for new readings.

FINN
Noted. But this is a decision for a human, not a program.

LIZZARDO
Aye, aye, Captain.

FINN
Hang on tight, we're halfway gone.

SPECIAL CLOSE-UP on FINN frowns, her concentration shaken. Then she closes her eyes and presses her hands together. The multicolored control lights expand and envelop her.

EXT. *BRAZILIA* - SPACE
The ship surges forward into the center of the open gate.

INT. *BRAZILIA* COCKPIT
Acceleration presses FINN into her seat. LIZZARDO is not affected. He leaps up and down, jabbing his fists in the air.

LIZZARDO
Yahoo!

FINN
(speaking with difficulty)
Better than the Planet-buster at Disneyworld Mars,
eh?

EXT. *BRAZILIA* - HYPERSPACE
The ship enters hyperspace, guided by the yellow ray.

INT. *BRAZILIA* COCKPIT
FINN sits unmoving in her control chair. Her face is tense,
slick with sweat; she's obviously mentally uncomfortable. On
her display, the beacon cuts through the stuff of hyperspace.
She breathes deeply, closes her eyes and cups her hands in her
lap as though meditating. She opens her eyes and smiles.

FINN
Let's–

FINN AND LIZZARDO
–impose a little order on chaos.

FINN makes a pistol-shooting gesture at the viewscreen.

On screen, the wild fabric of hyperspace folds back around the
yellow beacon, creating a corridor of calmness.

FINN
Smooth sailing from here, eh?

LIZZARDO
The beacon's at ninety-seven percent, but the ion flux
is nudging twenty...

Hyperspace suddenly convulses, as if shaken by a storm.

LIZZARDO
Make that thirty-three point six.

FINN
(sarcastically)
Great.

FINN makes passes among the control lights. Her face shows that she's taking this very seriously.

LIZZARDO
Beacon's at 85 percent. 72. No! It's coming back. 93 percent! 98 percent!

FINN
What the--

EXT. *BRAZILIA* - HYPERSPACE
The beacon buckles and distorts, then contorts into strange shapes. It shifts, coming from one direction, then another.

The beacon SNAPS like a rubber band stretched too far. The corridor collapses, engulfing the *Brazilia* in a hyperspace hurricane, a maelstrom of weirdness.

INT. *BRAZILIA* COCKPIT
Warning lights flash all over the cockpit. Alerts scroll across the viewscreen. A siren screams. The ship is buffeted from side to side. FINN almost falls from her seat; then restraints close around her.

LIZZARDO
We've lost the beacon!

FINN
Lock onto our last reading!

LIZZARDO
It's no good without a reference point!

FINN
Decelerating! If we can ride this out–

FINN does her damnedest to stabilize the ship, but fails. The *Brazilia* careens into hyperspace's uncharted depths.

LIZZARDO
Proximity alert! Jeez–incoming!

An enormous fiery shape hurtles directly at the viewscreen. As warning alarms blare, FINN screams, and...

MORPH TO:

INT. FINN'S BEDROOM - 1953 - DAWN
The FINN of the 1950s, the same young woman but with a period hairstyle, sits up in bed. Her face is twisted in terror.

Her apartment is a typical American middle-class urban one of the early 1950s. Out the window is a fire escape and a second-floor view of the nice downtown neighborhood of Roswell, New Mexico.

On her night table is a science-fiction paperback book titled *Nightspeeder*. The cover shows FINN as a Nightspeeder at the controls of her ship, screaming in terror. On the wall above is a 1953 calendar turned to April.

FINN recognizes the sound of the alarm from her dream–the black phone ringing on her night table. She shakes off her fear and answers it.

FINN
This better be good.

                    ZARDO (O.C.)
It's me.

                    FINN
The U.F.O. man?

                    ZARDO (O.C.)
Call me Zardo.

                    FINN
I'll call you Donald Duck if there's a story in it. You
sound pretty far away.

                    ZARDO (O.C.)
I'm—

DESERT PAY PHONE - DAWN
ZARDO is a small, dark-haired man in a slouch hat and a
trenchcoat. He appears in close-up; then the rest of the world
takes form around him. He's at a pay phone in front of a
country store in the desert. The Sun is rising.

                    ZARDO
—at a pay phone. You got my present?

INT. FINN'S APARTMENT - DAWN
FINN picks up the book and looks at the cover.

                    FINN
Yeah. Do people like this sci-fi crap?

INTERCUT PHONE CALL
                    ZARDO
It didn't tell you anything?

                    FINN
It's a little early for a book report, Mr. Zardo.

                    39

                    ZARDO
You don't find the truth working eight to five.

                    FINN
You don't find it in pulp fiction either. My editor
wants a series on flying saucers. Can you help, or do
I go back to sleep?

                    ZARDO
The story in the book is the key. Don't be distracted
from that.

                    FINN
Earning my paycheck is a distraction?

                    ZARDO
Your daily life is a trap. All that matters is finding
out what's going on.

FINN groans. This guy's a nut, just as she feared.

                    FINN
That's a very enlightened attitude, Mr. Zardo, but I'm
a worldly gal. If all you've got for me is a sci-fi
paperback, phone in a tip to the book review editor.

She hangs up firmly, looks at the book, then tosses it into the
bedside trash can.

EXT. *ROSWELL GUARDIAN* BUILDING - MORNING
FINN runs up the steps of the *Roswell Guardian* building. It's
in a prosperous small city in 1950s America: big lumpy tail-
finned cars, women in wide skirts, men in wide-shouldered
single-breasted suits.

INT. *GUARDIAN* OFFICES - DAY
FINN gets off the elevator.

                      40

DAN, a fellow reporter, waves a copy of the newspaper folded to show the saucer headline.

                    DAN
          Pulitzer Prize material, doll.

                    FINN
          Wait'll you see my next series. It's a hard-hitting
          exposé on the differences between cat owners and
          dog owners.

                    DAN
          Hey, you could still be assigned to hemline heights.

                    FINN
          Easy for you to say, Dan. You get to cover the House
          UnAmerican Activities Committee and Commie
          spies in Hollywood. I'm writing up people who see
          little green men.

                    DAN
               (looking at the paper)
          I thought Ralph wanted this played for laughs.

                    FINN
          Some of these U.F.O. kooks are pretty plausible. I
          hate to make them look like something they're not.

                    DAN
          Just make them entertaining. That's–

                    FINN
          –what sells papers. Yeah, yeah.

                              DAN
          Don't sweat it. You'll be off the nut beat and back on
          real news any day now.

INT. CIMINO'S OFFICE - DAY
FINN enters RALPH CIMINO's office, as PHIL JONAH, an
athletic man with a crew-cut, and two MEN IN BLACK
(white guys in black suits) leave.

Curious, FINN watches them go.

                              FINN
          What's up, Ralph?

                            CIMINO
          Let's take the U.F.O. series in a new direction.

                              FINN
          Oh?

                            CIMINO
          There's a darker side to this story, after all. Dark red.

                              FINN
          Communists?

                            CIMINO
          The country's finding 'em under every bush. Why
          not in the sky?

                              FINN
          You want me to write about Russians in flying
          saucers?

                            CIMINO
          I want something about who benefits from America's
          fascination with U.F.O.s.

FINN
Our newspaper?

CIMINO
It's not funny, Finn. Commies are among us.
McCarthy and Nixon are trying to make us wake up
and see that. But what do people want to read about?
Marsh gas. A drunk sees Venus on the horizon and
everybody says the Martians have landed.

FINN
People like novelty.

CIMINO
So let's give them some. Commies are creating these
flying saucer stories to divert attention from
themselves, get it?

FINN
I doubt the people I've interviewed are Commies.
They might sue if we suggested–

CIMINO
So they're Commie dupes. Hint that the Commies are
exploiting their beliefs.

FINN
You're signing my paychecks, Ralph.

INT. FINN'S DESK - DAY
FINN works at her typewriter. The phone rings.

FINN
Finn.

ZARDO (O.C.)
It's me.

43

FINN

Sorry, wrong number. This is the news desk. For the
fiction editor–

ZARDO (O.C.)

You're still working the U.F.O. story?

FINN

Not from the same angle, so there's nothing you can–

ZARDO (O.C.)

Angles change. I can still help you. Did you finish
the book I sent you?

FINN

I threw it away.

ZARDO (O.C.)

It's the key–

FINN

Is the author behind the U.F.O. scare?

ZARDO (O.C.)

You won't believe me if I tell you.

FINN

My job's to report, not to believe.

ZARDO (O.C.)

I can give you something to report.

FINN

Something I can't buy for twenty-five cents at a
newsstand? I want to know if someone's behind the
saucer scare.

ZARDO (O.C.)
That's what I want you to know.

FINN
Is there a connection between the saucer sightings
and the Communist conspiracy?

ZARDO (O.C.)
I'm offering you a major clue, Finn. Something you
can see and touch, if you dare. Meet me at midnight.

FINN glances around the office, then makes up her mind.

FINN
Where?

EXT. AIR FORCE BASE PERIMETER - NIGHT
A sign on a high chain-link fence reads, "KEEP OUT! GOV-
ERNMENT PROPERTY," followed by several lines too small
to read. Nearby, FINN stands by her car parked on a dirt road.

A plane roars overhead. FINN looks up. When she looks
down, she's surprised to see ZARDO in hat and trenchcoat.

FINN
Mr. Zardo?

ZARDO
Yes.

FINN
Where's your car?

ZARDO
We can't take cars where we're going.

                    FINN
We're sneaking onto the base? It's a federal offense.

                    ZARDO
I didn't think you'd be afraid. At least, I didn't think
that would hold you back.

                    FINN
     It won't.

ZARDO pulls at a fence post, and a section of fence rolls
back. ZARDO slips through.

FINN follows. ZARDO closes the fence behind them.

They walk through the darkness. ZARDO suddenly grabs
FINN and pulls her down.

A jeep drives by, patrolling the fence line. After it passes,
ZARDO stands up.

                    FINN
     You know what you're doing?

ZARDO looks at her.

                    FINN
     Yeah, it's a little late for that question. Let's go.

EXT. AIR FORCE BASE - NIGHT
FINN and ZARDO run across a wide area of concrete to
crouch beside a building. Two armed U.S. SOLDIERS walk
by.

When the soldiers pass, FINN and ZARDO run to a building
labelled "HANGAR 18." FINN breathes hard; ZARDO
doesn't.

ZARDO

Come on.

ZARDO leads FINN around the corner of the building. ZARDO opens the door and steps aside to let FINN enter.

INT. HANGAR 18 HALLWAY - NIGHT
ZARDO

I'll play sentry until you get back. Don't take your time.

FINN

Which way?

ZARDO

Straight ahead.

FINN

What am I looking for?

ZARDO

You'll know it when you see it.

ZARDO goes out. FINN walks down the hall and opens a door.

INT. HANGAR 18 MAIN ROOM - NIGHT
FINN steps into a huge room. Inside is a strange-looking spaceship that seems to have been half-devoured... but by what? It resembles the front end of the *Brazilia*.

FINN takes a camera out of her purse and circles the ship, taking photographs.

An ALARM sounds. FINN starts, and runs for the door.

INT. HANGAR 18 HALLWAY - NIGHT
FINN runs for the door. ZARDO looks in.

> ZARDO
> Hurry!

> FINN
> There's a thought.

EXT. AIR FORCE BASE - NIGHT
FINN runs outside. ZARDO catches her arm, and they walk down the sidewalk.

A jeep arrives, driven by a MILITARY POLICEMAN.

> M.P.
> What's going on?

> ZARDO
> Probably a false alarm.

ZARDO grabs the M.P. and yanks him out of the jeep.

> ZARDO
> Get in!

FINN and ZARDO scramble into the jeep, ZARDO in the driver's seat. The M.P. runs toward them, opening his holster as he runs.

> M.P.
> Halt!

ZARDO sits perfectly still.

> FINN
> Don't tell me you can't drive.

ZARDO

Internal combustion engine. Jeep. Yes.

The jeep lunges away, past a fire truck bound for Hangar 18.

<u>EXT. AIR FORCE BASE AIR FIELD - NIGHT</u>

The jeep races across the field. FINN looks back. Another jeep
pursues them, M.P.s clinging to its side.

FINN

Why'd I do this?

ZARDO

Because you have to know.

FINN

I don't have to know what twenty years in
Leavenworth is like.

The jeep leaves the pavement. ZARDO drives over rocky,
brush-covered ground.

ZARDO

Relax. That's not a likely outcome.

FINN

What is a likely outcome?

ZARDO

There are only two. Escape, or death.

FINN

I feel much better. What was that ... thing? In the
hangar?

ZARDO

You don't know?

FINN
It looked like somebody's nightmare.

Realizing what she's said, she looks at ZARDO.

ZARDO
Precisely.

FINN
Who are you?

The jeep is blocked by an outcrop of large rocks. ZARDO
brings it screeching to a halt.

ZARDO
Someone who can help you.

FINN studies ZARDO. Then she hears soldiers running toward them, and she leaps out of the jeep.

FINN
Later! Come on!

EXT. AIR FORCE BASE PERIMETER - NIGHT
FINN pushes through the fence and runs toward her car.

FINN
What now?

FINN looks back...and finds ZARDO gone. She hears the soldiers coming close. She starts her car and roars away.

EXT. HIGHWAY - NIGHT
FINN rounds a curve in the highway.

Two military trucks block the road, flanked by SOLDIERS with rifles. With them are JONAH and two MEN IN BLACK.

In the rear-view mirror, FINN sees a military jeep behind her: she's trapped.

<u>INT. HANGAR 18 FRONT HALLWAY - NIGHT</u>
JONAH and the two M.I.B.s escort FINN into the hangar. JONAH carries FINN's camera.

> FINN
> Am I under arrest, or not?

> JONAH
> Why? What've you done?

JONAH opens the door to the main room. FINN stares in, then enters.

<u>INT. HANGAR 18 MAIN ROOM - NIGHT</u>
The room is empty. FINN turns around once, staring.

> FINN
> Where'd you move it?

> JONAH
> Move what?

> FINN
> The ship.

> JONAH
> Ship? This is an Air Force base. It's a bit of a walk to the sea.

> FINN
> The space ship.

                    JONAH
        Are you sure you feel all right?

                    FINN
        You moved it. I want to see–

A M.I.B. blocks her way.

                    JONAH
        This is a top secret military installation. I'm showing
        you this room out of respect for the press. There's no
        story here, Finn.

                    FINN
        I saw it.

                    JONAH
        What?

                    FINN
        A ... space ship. Some kind of alien flying machine.

                    JONAH
        Do you have proof?

JONAH opens her camera and pulls out the film, exposing it.

                    FINN
        Guess not. You can't stop me from telling my story.

                    JONAH
        Actually, we could. But it's easier just to see that no
        one believes it.

EXT. HIGHWAY - NIGHT
JONAH and the M.I.B.s drive FINN in a black car.

INT. JONAH'S CAR - NIGHT

                    JONAH
          You don't know how to reach this man you call
          Zardo?

                    FINN
          He calls himself Zardo. I wouldn't call him if he gave
          me the nickel. He got in touch with me claiming to be
          some kind of U.F.O. expert.

                    JONAH
          And you fell for it?

                    FINN
          I didn't fall for anything. I asked him for information.

                    JONAH
          And he enlisted your help in stealing U.S. military
          secrets.

                    FINN
          What military secrets?

                    JONAH
          I'm afraid that's classified.

                    FINN
          Do they involve the space ship I didn't see?

                    JONAH
          That would be impossible, wouldn't it?

                    FINN
          Darn.

                        JONAH
        Commies try to draw good Americans into their web
        of intrigue. It certainly helped his cause this time. We
        caught you, and he got away.

                        FINN
        If this has to do with Communists, where does the
        space ship come in?

JONAH's car approaches the site where FINN was stopped.

                        JONAH
        Off the record, that damaged plane is a highly
        classified U.S. project. I trust you to keep it quiet and
        help us catch this "Zardo."

JONAH stops next to FINN's car. She gets out. JONAH hands
her a card.

                        JONAH
        Call us if you hear from him.

                        FINN
        Of course.

FINN watches JONAH drive away.

EXT. FINN'S APARTMENT - NIGHT
The streets are deserted. FINN enters her building. In the sky,
unnoticed by her, a light hovers, then streaks away.

INT. CIMINO'S OFFICE - THE NEXT DAY
FINN sits with a cup of coffee, listening to RALPH CIMINO.

CIMINO
You've got no evidence. This Zardo guy's
disappeared. And you want me to run a story on the
Air Force's U.F.O.?

FINN
If we put pressure on them—

CIMINO
Finn. We run a lot of fluff in this rag. Maybe the
U.F.O. series was a mistake. But it was supposed to
expose the whole thing as hysteria.

FINN
There's something there.

CIMINO
You've got nothing. You're a good reporter, but
you've got nothing.

FINN
Give me time.

CIMINO
Finn, I like you. You know that.

FINN
I didn't, but I'm glad to hear it.

CIMINO
Good. So if I ask you to see someone, for your own
good, you would, right?

FINN
What are you talking about, Ralph?

RALPH hands a business card to FINN. She reads it.

                    FINN
          Dr. Yarrow? I had a physical–

                    CIMINO
          He's a psychiatrist, Finn.

                    FINN
          There's nothing wrong with me.

                    CIMINO
          Everyone needs a rest now and then. Dan can finish
          your series. It'll tie in with his story about the
          Hollywood Eight.

                    FINN
          I don't need time off.

                    CIMINO
          See Yarrow. Then we'll talk more.

                    FINN
                 (coldly)
          Right.

FINN stalks out.

INT. _GUARDIAN_ OFFICES - DAY
As FINN leaves CIMINO's office, DAN passes in the hall.
RALPH opens his office door.

                    CIMINO
          Hey, Dan. Got a minute?

                    DAN
          Sure. Excuse me, Finn.

FINN stalks to the water cooler and fills a Dixie cup. She walks back past RALPH's office, where his silhouette and DAN's are visible on the frosted glass of the door.

She overhears RALPH and DAN talking in RUSSIAN WITHOUT SUBTITLES. She stops, shocked. Then someone taps FINN on the shoulder. She turns. It's RALPH'S SECRETARY.

> SECRETARY
> I set up an appointment with Dr. Yarrow for you. He can see you this afternoon.

> FINN
> Oh. Sure. Thanks.

FINN looks around the office. No one meets her eye.

INT. DR. YARROW'S OFFICE - DAY
DR. YARROW is an older man with an unidentifiable European accent. His office looks like a rich man's library. FINN lies on a classic psychiatrist's couch. YARROW sits nearby.

> YARROW
> These, ah, men in black, they did not identify themselves?

> FINN
> Could've been F.B.I., C.I.A., Secret Service or dog catchers. It doesn't really matter, does it?

> YARROW
> What you think matters a great deal.

> FINN
> Do you think I'm nuts?

YARROW

"Nuts" is not a useful term.

FINN

How about paranoid? Delusional? Schizophrenic?
Irrational?

YARROW

I think your research into U.F.O.s has made you
vulnerable to the very paranoia that you set out to
expose.

FINN

I'm a reporter. I don't fall for everything I'm told.

YARROW

As a woman in an unfeminine career, you are
naturally insecure. You compensate with pride and
recklessness, but this compensation cannot be
sustained forever. Some sort of breakdown was
inevitable.

FINN

I'm not insecure.

YARROW

This is only my hypothesis.

FINN

I have a better one. I saw a space ship. Men in black
removed the evidence. But you're right, it sounds
crazy.

YARROW

So you have doubts about your, ah, experience?

                    FINN
         Why would the government keep that kind of secret?
         Unless it has something to do with fighting the war in
         Korea.

YARROW goes to his desk and opens a drawer.

                    YARROW
         These speculations only agitate you. I have
         something to help you relax.

YARROW offers her a bottle of large, evil-looking red capsules.

                    YARROW
         Take two before every meal.

                    FINN
         You do think I'm nuts.

                    YARROW
         I think everyone is a little nuts. There's no shame in
         accepting help.

FINN accepts the bottle of pills.

                    FINN
         I–You know best, Doc.

EXT. ROSWELL STREETS - EVENING
Outside, FINN throws the pills into a trash can. She looks up
and sees an unmarked black car pass slowly by.

Walking home, she spots a MAN IN BLACK reflected in a
store window. He's following half a block behind. She looks
back.

The M.I.B. smiles at FINN. She whirls and walks on.

INT. FINN'S LIVING ROOM - NIGHT
FINN enters her apartment and turns on a light. She gasps.
ZARDO is waiting for her.

                    ZARDO
          I'm not supposed to be here.

                    FINN
          You just saved me a line.

                    ZARDO
          They'll get me, if they can.

                    FINN
          I might be inclined to help them. Who're "they"?

                    ZARDO
          The forces behind this. Don't trust Yarrow.

                    FINN
          He's one of them?

                    ZARDO
          He may be in charge, or only another puppet.

                    FINN
          Are you a Commie?

                    ZARDO
               (laughing)
          No.

                    FINN
          You skipped out on me last night.

ZARDO

I don't know what they'll do if they catch me. I don't
dare find out.

FINN

I see you have my interests at heart.

ZARDO

Without me, you can't get out of this.

FINN

Sure I can. I can take Yarrow's happy pills, go back
to work and forget the whole thing.

ZARDO

Then people will die, while you go on, blind to
what's happening around you.

FINN

Or I can keep snooping. On my own.

ZARDO

You need me, Finn. They can create webs of intrigue
that you'll never penetrate. Secrets within mysteries
within conundrums within enigmas within lies.

FINN

With a side of bullshit. What's going on?

ZARDO

You're not ready for it.

FINN

There's a government conspiracy? That's easy. I saw
an honest-to-God alien space ship? Tougher, but
I would consider it.

ZARDO

Come with me. We'll make them reveal themselves.

There is a KNOCK at the door.

JONAH

Open up!

FINN looks at ZARDO.

ZARDO

They'll break the door down if you don't.

ZARDO heads for the bedroom. FINN opens the door. JO-
NAH and two M.I.B.s enter, pushing past her.

JONAH

Mind if we come in?

FINN

I guess not.

JONAH

And take a look around?

JONAH motions for the other two to search the place.

FINN

Yes, damn it, I mind!

FINN starts after the M.I.B.s. JONAH grabs her arm.

JONAH

What're you hiding?

FINN

Don't I have a right to privacy?

                            JONAH
          So long as we can convict you of espionage, you
          don't have any rights at all.

One M.I.B. heads into the bathroom. The other enters the bedroom. FINN pulls free and runs after him.

INT. FINN'S BEDROOM - NIGHT
As FINN enters, the only person in the room is the M.I.B.
looking into her closet. JONAH follows FINN.

                            FINN
                 What're you looking for?

                            JONAH
              Mr. Zardo may be in the area.

The window is slightly open. JONAH opens it further and
looks out. No one is on the fire escape. The alley is empty.

                            JONAH
          But then, you would've reported to us if he had been.

INT. FINN'S LIVING ROOM - NIGHT
FINN, JONAH and one M.I.B. rejoin the other.

                            JONAH
          Anything?

The second M.I.B. shakes his head. JONAH jerks his head
toward the door. The M.I.B.s leave. JONAH pauses.

                            JONAH
          Dr. Yarrow's real name is Yarovitov. He may be part
          of a network stealing atomic secrets for Russia. You
          might keep an eye on him for us.

FINN
Aren't I doing you enough favors?

JONAH
You can never do enough favors for your friends.

JONAH leaves. FINN runs to the bedroom.

INT. FINN'S BEDROOM - NIGHT
FINN stops in the middle of the room.

FINN
Zardo?

She peers out the window. The alley is empty. She looks up into the night sky. A flying saucer hovers overhead, then zooms away.

INT. DR. YARROW'S OFFICE - DAY
FINN is on the couch, talking with DR. YARROW.

FINN
Yarrow's an interesting name.

YARROW
I shortened it to a good American name when
I became a good American. You still seem troubled.
The pills did not help?

FINN
They–

Through the window, FINN sees a U.F.O. hovering. As soon as she sees it, it whisks away.

YARROW
What's wrong?

                    FINN
        I don't–Nothing.

                    YARROW
    Here.

YARROW offers her a glass of water and two red capsules.
FINN hesitates, then nods and takes them.

EXT. ROSWELL STREETS - EVENING
FINN walks in a daze, ignoring the black car following her,
the U.F.O.s in the sky. PEOPLE on the street walk past FINN,
chatting to each other in Russian.

The black car pulls up beside her. ZARDO, inside, opens the
door.

                    ZARDO
        Get in.

                    FINN
        I'm going crazy.

                    ZARDO
    You've been crazy. It's time to go sane.

FINN gets into the passenger seat.

INT. ZARDO'S CAR - EVENING
ZARDO hands FINN a copy of the *Nightspeeder* paperback.

                    ZARDO
        You're ready. Here.

                    FINN
        No.

                    ZARDO
If you can only get the truth as fiction, then get it that
way.

                    FINN
I get sick if I read in the car.

                    ZARDO
No jokes, Finn. The answer's in that book. It's the
only way I can get it to you.

                    FINN
I read the beginning. It had nothing to do with
conspiracies, Commies or U.F.O.s. It's some
futuristic disaster–

                    ZARDO
That's right.

                    FINN
You think the U.F.O.s are from 2092?

ZARDO looks in the rear-view mirror. Headlights approach
rapidly.

                    ZARDO
I should've known it wouldn't be easy.

EXT. ZARDO'S CAR - COUNTRY ROADS - NIGHT
ZARDO's car is chased along back roads by another black car,
driven by JONAH with his M.I.B.s.

INT. ZARDO'S CAR - NIGHT
                    FINN
Where're we going?

ZARDO
To beat them at their own game.

FINN looks at the book. Her hand trembling, she lifts it into the glare of JONAH's lights and stares at the cover.

EXT. ZARDO'S CAR - COUNTRY ROADS - NIGHT
ZARDO takes a curve and whips onto a side road. He kills the lights. JONAH's black sedan speeds past the turnoff.

A beam of light from a U.F.O. shines down on FINN and ZARDO's car. ZARDO loses control and crashes into a ditch.

EXT. THE MIDDLE OF NOWHERE - NIGHT
FINN and ZARDO stagger from the wreckage, scratched but otherwise unhurt. Their car catches fire.

JONAH's sedan pulls up behind them. JONAH and his M.I.B.s get out. FINN looks from them to the hovering U.F.O.

FINN
The government's working with the U.F.O.s!
Is that it?

ZARDO shakes his head sadly.

The U.F.O. lands. A door opens, and Dr. YARROW steps out.

YARROW
(to Finn)
You've been through a trying experience. But I can still help you.

YARROW holds out another bottle of red pills.

YARROW
All will be restored, if you submit.

67

FINN backs away. She looks from JONAH to YARROW, to
ZARDO.

                    FINN
     I don't trust any of you!

                    ZARDO
     Think, Finn! You can find conspiracies within
     conspiracies forever! There's got to be one straight
     answer!

                    YARROW
                (to Zardo)
     You do not know how to play.

                    JONAH
                (to Finn)
     Zardo's not your friend.

                    YARROW
                (to Finn)
     What he wants frightens you, doesn't it?

                    ZARDO
     The truth is always frightening, Finn!

A M.I.B. reaches for FINN's arm. She twists away.

                    FINN
     This isn't right!

                    YARROW
                (to Zardo)
     You have spoiled it.

To FINN's horror, JONAH and the M.I.B. transform into ghastly demon-like aliens, long-tongued robotic creatures–the RAKASHAS.

YARROW changes into something hellish and horrible, a skull-headed manifestation of the being called YAMA.

FINN

No!

The creatures swarm over FINN and ZARDO and...

MORPH TO:

INT. NEW YORK - GAMING ARCADE - 2081 – DAY
The arcade is a flat-lit room with rows of VR stations occupied by PLAYERS of various ages. Piped-in dance music competes with the sounds from the stations.

Each station has a treadmill that moves in any direction, a railing with infrared transmitters and receivers, and a screen displaying the score and game status. Players wear wireless helmets and are covered with a grid of light–the infrared control system monitoring their movement.

FINN, age 16, is at a station whose viewscreen advertises a game called "ROSWELL-'53." The graphics look like the art in the previous section of this story.

She yanks off her helmet. Her face is soaked with sweat, and still twisted with fear. She looks down at the score display. It reads, "YOU DIED. GAME OVER."

Her best friend, NICKY, is at the next station. His helmet's on, and he's traced all over with the lights of the infrared grid. From his motions, he's snowboarding. FINN reaches over and yanks at his sleeve.

FINN
Nicky! Mutant! Drop out of it, pod-head!

NICKY's arms flail as he loses his balance. He slips and sits down hard. The infrared grid shuts off.

He pulls off his helmet and looks mournfully up at FINN.

NICKY
It was my personal best, Finn. I could see the finish line. The crowd was going wild.

FINN
Somebody hacked "Roswell-'53"–I got vacuumed on level five!

NICKY
You're getting old. Losing your edge.

FINN
I was eaten by a bunch of aliens who aren't part of the game!

NICKY
If they aren't part of the game, how could they be in the game?

FINN
Nicky, I'm the Supreme Ruler of "Roswell-'53." I've surfed level 12 and lived. This game has no aliens that look like anteaters in tin cans.

NICKY
(admiringly)
Dense. D'you think it'd do it for me?

FINN

You don't want it to. It was... it was kind of scary,
actually.

EXT. NEW YORK STREETS - DAY

New York City at Christmastime 2081 is overcrowded,
shabby, loud, garish and hectic–but exciting and attractive to a
confident teenager. New buildings tower over older ones like
the Chrysler Building.

Pedestrian walkways connect buildings at many levels. Mass
transit pods zip above the street, their single guide rails
stacked so that three pod routes can run in the same street.

The street and sky are full of ghostly 3-D ads and shows that
seem projected from nowhere on the air itself: "atmosvids."

The streets are crammed with SHOPPERS. When ads get in
their way, the shoppers walk through them. One atmosvid
advertises a dealer in flying "cars": "CLOSEOUT ON ALL
2081 MODELS! See the '82 Icarus Sport Coupe!"

FINN and NICKY leave a building painted with 20-foot-high
game characters. A sign over the door reads, "CYBERBUL-
LET VRcade." Gusts of wind tug at their clothes; the sky is
grey.

NICKY

I bet it was haunted.

FINN

What?

A woman's face two stories high appears in the air over the
sidewalk. Her eye makeup and lipstick are bright blue, blue
gloves grace the hands she raises to her silver-blue hair.

71

FEMALE AD VOICE
You'll want blue in '82. Flashmag. Get the picture.

FINN and NICKY walk through the ad image, ignoring it.

NICKY
That VR station. It's probably haunted by the ghost
of somebody who died at it.

FINN
(laughing)
You fell on your butt, not your head.

Four KIDS FINN's age stand on the other side of the street.
One of them notices FINN and NICKY and waves.

KID ON STREET
Finn! Hi!

The other three kids look up, grin and wave at FINN and
NICKY. FINN waves back as she and NICKY walk on.

NICKY
It's true! People have heart attacks during the game.
Their ghosts haunt the station and try to kill the next
player. I saw it on the atmosvids.

FINN
Atmosvid's vapor. Atmosvid news is full of stuff like
"Aliens kidnap President and replace her with
Bigfoot."

NICKY points to an atmosvid ad overhead. In it, LIZZARDO
battles an army of human-sized, funny-looking RATS, using
cartoon martial arts moves.

NICKY
"Lizzardo" is not vapor.

FINN
"Lizzardo" is dense and intense. OK, atmosvid's not totally vapor. But otherwise, stick to the persvid, Mutant.

NICKY
Uh, my persvid privileges are kinda... suspended.

FINN winces.

FINN
Calculus again?

NICKY
My grades are at the bottom of the gravity well.

FINN
Come over to my place and we can study.

NICKY
Don't you have to work?

FINN
Oh, gas me! Come on–I'll be late!

EXT. FINN'S APARTMENT BUILDING - DAY
FINN and NICKY arrive, panting, at FINN's apartment building. The building is comfortable and middle-class. The street is quieter here, but still busy.

NICKY
I'll just, you know, wait down here.

FINN
I don't need anything from upstairs. Why are you
afraid of my dad?

NICKY
I'm not! Not exactly.

They hurry down an alley to a row of small garage doors.

FINN
Not exactly not afraid?

FINN presses her thumb to the lock on a door. The light above
the lock changes from red to green. She opens the door.

NICKY
He always gives me that look. "So, young man, have
you won a Nobel Prize yet? No? Then why are you
here?"

In the garage is an airbike–a flying motorcycle. It's old, with
scratched paint and mismatched parts.

FINN rolls it out of the storage room. She takes a helmet off a
hook on the wall.

FINN
Dad's not that bad. He expects a lot, but he's really
sweet. Want a ride home?

NICKY
You'd be late for work.

FINN
Not if you come along on my route and I drop you
off after.

NICKY

Can you?

FINN

A lot of the riders do it.

FINN starts the bike. NICKY grabs a second helmet from the wall, slams the garage door and hops on behind her.

NICKY

Good. I forgot to renew my transit pass.

FINN

You were going to walk home? You're lucky I'm here to take care of you.

EXT. NEW YORK SKIES - DAY

FINN and NICKY zip into the crowded sky on FINN's air-bike, hurrying to beat the weather.

NICKY

We're both lucky. I give your life meaning–

FINN zig-zags. NICKY grabs for her waist.

NICKY

Whoa! I take it back!

FINN

I thought you would.

NICKY

Seriously, we're frozen-solid lucky. I'll be the world's greatest game designer–

FINN

And the most humble.

75

NICKY
–and you'll be the most famous star pilot ever.

FINN
(laughing)
When I tell reporters I used to deliver packages,
they'll say, "Gee, couldn't you find anything sloggier
to do?"

NICKY
You scoff now, but you'll see.

EXT. COURIER SERVICE BIKE BARN - DAY
FINN and NICKY, on the airbike, fly through the doors of the
warehouse-like bike barn. It's where couriers collect their parcels and load their bikes. There's a workbench on one side,
and a terminal where couriers log on and receive their packages and route information.

Signs on the wall: "Safety first and last!" "Company Rules:"
(followed by columns of unreadable text). "If they want it late,
they can use our competitors." "CARRYING PASSENGERS
STRICTLY FORBIDDEN!"

INT. COURIER SERVICE - DISPATCH OFFICE
On the wall is a poster of a new airbike. Next to it is a display
board reading: "COURIER OF THE YEAR WINS THIS 2082
VELOS CHEETAH AIRBIKE!"

Beneath that is the line, "COURIER YEAR-TO-DATE REC-
ORD," and a list of names, with delivery and on-time statis-
tics. FINN is at the top with 3032. Next is SARAI, with 3028.

The dispatcher, BENNY, sits behind a counter. He's college-
age, interestingly dressed. He wears headphones. Eyes closed,
he bobs his head to the rhythm of whatever he's listening to.

                    FINN
    Hey, Benny.

Benny keeps bobbing. FINN sighs, rolls her eyes. NICKY
grins. FINN waves her hand in front of Benny's face.

                    FINN
    Benny!

FINN pulls one of the earpieces away from Benny's ear.

                    FINN
    BENNY!

                    BENNY
    Jeez, don't do that!

                    FINN
    How do you answer the phones?

                    BENNY
    I patched the ringers into the headphones.

                    FINN
    What if the boss walks in?

                    BENNY
    I set up a motion sensor over his parking space. It
    interrupts the audio signal with an alarm.

                    NICKY
    That's a lot of work to keep from working.

                    FINN
    So log me on, Captain Ben.

BENNY
Have you seen the weather forecast? Looks like you
get tonight off, Finn.

FINN
What? It's hardly raining!

NICKY looks outside. The rain is coming down heavily.

NICKY
Actually, it's raining hardly.

FINN
It'll clear.

BENNY
Nope. Weather Control says it's some kind of mutant
Atlantic thunderstorm.

Benny swings his monitor around to show FINN. It displays
several "windows." One lists couriers out on deliveries, and
their destinations and parcels. Another is a music video.

The upper display shows a weather radar map of Manhattan
Island, captioned, "WEATHER CONTROL SEVERE
WEATHER WATCH."

WEATHER VOICE
...small vehicle warning above fifteen kilometers due
to gusting winds. Rain possibly mixed with hail by
evening. Visibility dropping to zero in...

BENNY
I'm supposed to close the office in half an hour. I'll
have to call the riders in.

FINN
Let me see that screen again.

FINN looks at the list of couriers on duty. Sarai's name is on it. She looks up at the wall display of couriers' totals.

FINN
Weather Control's never right.

BENNY
Don't, Finn. I won't log you on.

FINN
Please? Just for half an hour. I can do all my deliveries before you call us in.

BENNY
You won't get me in trouble?

FINN
Word of honor, Captain.

INT. COURIER SERVICE - BIKE BARN
FINN loads four parcels into the storage space on her bike. NICKY watches, frowning.

NICKY
If I were you, Mutant, I'd have been halfway home before he finished saying, "You get the night off."

FINN
Sarai is four deliveries behind me. If I go home now, she'll be ahead. What if I can't catch up?

NICKY
You're doing this to win a bike?

FINN finishes loading. She doesn't look at NICKY.

> FINN
> I haven't told my dad about the competition. If I
> come home with that bike, he'll be so proud of me...

> NICKY
> Why shouldn't he be proud of you already?

An airbike swoops in and lands beside FINN's. The paint is
scraped off this bike on one side. Bike and rider are soaked.

The rider pulls off her dripping helmet. It's SARAI.

> FINN
> Hey, Sarai. What kept you?

> SARAI
> You're not going out now?

> FINN
> No, I thought I'd do figure eights in here. I'm not
> afraid to get wet.

> SARAI
> (surveying Finn's bike)
> I understand your desperation.

FINN, mildly affronted, pats the saddle of her bike.

> FINN
> Hey, we may not be the latest and greatest, but we get
> the job done.

> NICKY
> (studiedly innocent)
> Better than anyone, I hear.

SARAI

Well, mind the wind when you and old Dobbin there
head out.
(pointing to scrape on bike)
I scraped a pylon and lost a package.

FINN

You lost a package? Benny'll cut off your ears and
hang them in Dispatch as a warning!

SARAI

It could happen to you, Princess.

Sarai pushes her bike away, then turns to FINN and grins.

SARAI

I'm three deliveries ahead now.

FINN
(nodding toward Nicky)
I'm packing my good-luck charm. Don't polish those
new fenders yet!

Sarai heads for the dispatch office to log out. NICKY cranes
his neck to look out at the weather.

NICKY

What's the matter, do you think your good-luck
charm needs a bath?

FINN

Have faith. We'll go so fast even raindrops won't
catch us.

FINN mounts the bike and puts her helmet on.

                         FINN
              Unless you want to stay behind?

                         NICKY
              Vapor, no, not if you're going.

NICKY gets on behind FINN and puts on the spare helmet.

                         FINN
              I'll take care of you. Hang on tight, we're halfway
              gone!

SAME CLOSE-UP AS BEFORE: A puzzled look crosses
FINN's face. She shakes it off.

EXT. NEW YORK STREETS & SKIES - LATE AFTER-
NOON
Rain and wind lash the airbike.

                         FINN
              Saint Francis Hospital–this one's easy.

The bike drops down and levels off at second-floor level.

                         NICKY
              Wha-hoo!

The emergency room entrance looms ahead. FINN dodges a
parked ambulance and pulls a box out of the storage space.

An ORDERLY dives out the door and waves.

                         FINN
              Right on time!

She tosses the box. The orderly catches it, grins, gives her a
thumbs-up. FINN peels off into the sky.

EXT. ELSEWHERE BOOKS - DAY

As FINN and NICKY rocket toward the bookstore, wind slams into the bike. The bike sideslips toward the wall.

FINN heads the bike into the wind and drops the nose. It settles to the pavement inches from the wall.

NICKY leaps off the bike. FINN tosses him the package, and he runs for the door of the bookstore.

FINN looks at the sky. The storm is gathering force. FINN frowns, then grins as NICKY comes out of the store, laughing as he slides across the wet pavement.

EXT. MONUMENT INSURANCE BUILDING - DAY

FINN and NICKY are soaked; for a moment, it's hard to see. The insurance company building looms up out of the rain.

                    NICKY
     Aaagh!

                    FINN
          Under control, Nicky-boy.

FINN climbs, racing up the face of the building, and lands on the roof among several vehicles like flying limousines.

A WOMAN IN A SUIT waits in the door to the elevators. She smiles as she takes the package from NICKY.

FINN and NICKY take to the air.

EXT. STREETS OF NEW YORK - DAY

A bolt of lightning ricochets between the tallest buildings.

                    FINN
          That's enough! Let's head back.

NICKY
Hot chocolate is calling my name.

FINN
Since when is your name "Finn"?

An air-taxi rounds the corner of the building ahead, barely visible through the driving rain. It's going much too fast.

NICKY

FINN!

FINN

Hang on!

FINN slams the throttle and yanks the bike's nose up. It stalls.

The taxi is so close that the driver's panic-stricken face shows in the windshield. The taxi veers, but not far enough.

Then the bike shoots nearly straight up. It misses the taxi by maybe a finger's width.

FINN struggles to level off against a gust of wind. NICKY looks back and down, where the taxi dwindles behind them.

NICKY
(thrilled)
Dense and intense! Better than virtual!

FINN sees shapes ahead in the rain: a row of polished steel gargoyles decorating the roofline of a building.

FINN
NICKY! Get down!

FINN hunches forward over the handgrips as the shining beak of the first gargoyle comes at her.

NICKY

What–

The beak passes over FINN's head and strikes NICKY in the chest. The force of the blow breaks his seat belt.

NICKY falls the long, long way toward the street.

FINN

No! Nooo!

FINN U-turns the bike and plunges downward. She's two stories from the street when even she can see it's too late.

PEDESTRIANS below are converging on the disaster. Vehicles are stopping, landing. In the distance a siren howls.

Hovering on the bike, FINN covers her face and screams.

<u>INT. NEW YORK POLICE STATION - NIGHT</u>
FINN, pale, damp and disheveled, huddles in a chair, watched by a stern COP. She seems very small and isolated.

The station is noisy, with phones ringing, lots of PEOPLE talking, some yelling, the DISPATCHER rattling off the locations of cruisers and officers' reports. It's all a distant buzz...until one voice penetrates FINN's fog.

FINN'S FATHER

...I've come to pick up my daughter.

Before the stern cop can stop her, FINN runs toward her FATHER, who's talking to a DESK COP at the front counter.

                         FINN
          Dad!

Her FATHER stretches out his arms... and grabs her by the
shoulders, stopping her before she can reach him.

                         FINN
          Dad? I... Nicky and I...

                    FINN'S FATHER
          The police called me at the office. They told me what
          happened.
                    (to the desk cop)
          May I take her home now?

                       DESK COP
          Yes, sir. We've taken her statement.

                    FINN'S FATHER
          Statement?

                       DESK COP
          She'll have to appear before the juvenile court judge
          tomorrow morning at nine.

                    FINN'S FATHER
          I see. Thank you.

FINN and her FATHER turn away from the desk. FINN'S
FATHER leans over her, frowning.

                    FINN'S FATHER
          You gave them a statement? My God, I'm going to
          have to admit to the partners that my own daughter
          waived her right to have an attorney present.

                              FINN
          I called you. Your secretary said you were in a
          meeting.

As they reach the door, an officer escorts a man and woman
into the room. They're MR. and MRS. DICKS, NICKY's parents. They look dazed; both have been crying.

                              FINN
          Mr. and Mrs. Dicks–I'm sorry about Nicky. I'm
          really...

The DICKS walk past, seeming not to notice her. FINN'S
FATHER pulls her out of the room.

EXT. FINN'S APARTMENT BUILDING - NIGHT
The rain's still falling. A ground taxi delivers FINN and her
father to the front door of the building.

INT. FINN'S LIVING ROOM - NIGHT
The living room is small, functional, but not cozy. Christmas
cards stand on a table; they're the only holiday decorations.
The crowded New York skyline is visible through the windows.

FINN and her father enter. He hangs up his coat and walks
over to a chair, picks up the paper and sits down.

FINN looks after him wistfully. She hangs up her own coat
and comes to stand beside his chair.

                              FINN
          Dad?

                              FINN'S FATHER
          Yes.

FINN
Dad, please talk to me.

FINN'S FATHER
Isn't that what I'm doing?

FINN
If you're mad at me, say so! Yell at me!

FINN'S FATHER
Did you do this thing so that I would yell at you?

FINN
Of course not!

FINN'S FATHER
It makes as much sense as anything else. I can't
understand how my daughter could have been so
criminally irresponsible.

FINN
It was an accident.

FINN'S FATHER
I said "irresponsible," didn't I?

FINN
The taxi driver was speeding and in my air lane. The
witnesses said so. They said I did everything I could–

FINN'S FATHER
And did you?

FINN can't answer. This is exactly what haunts her.

FINN'S FATHER
Is that how you display responsibility? By blaming
others for your bad judgment?

FINN
I wasn't blaming–

FINN'S FATHER
I thought you understood when you got your license
that being a driver means expecting the unexpected.
Apparently I was mistaken.

FINN
Dad, please! I'm sorry–

FINN'S FATHER
That won't bring your friend back.

A few tears run down FINN's cheeks.

FINN
No. Nothing will do that.

FINN turns and runs for her bedroom.

Her father stares blindly over his paper. FINN's door slams.
He closes his eyes. He looks hurt, confused... and sad.

INT. FINN'S BEDROOM - NIGHT
FINN's room is full of photo posters and models of space-
ships, aircraft and airbikes. Over the bed, near a cluttered
dressing table, is a poster of LIZZARDO.

On the dressing table is a persvid unit, a box that can display a
3-D image in the air above it. There's a desk with a computer,
books, infodisks and wireless headphones.

There's a half-finished shuttlecraft model on a shelf. Beside it is an eight-inch high Lizzardo action figure.

FINN picks up a remote control and points it at the persvid box. An image springs to life above it: two Adventurers help each other scale a cliff.

FINN changes channels. A World War I aerial battle: one plane fires, hits another, which pinwheels toward the ground. She clicks again and gets an episode of "Lizzardo."

In a post-holocaust desert landscape, two RATS fight over a very small, pitiful-looking, humanoid FEMALE.

> RAT 1 (ON PERSVID)
> I'm gonna eat her! I saw her first!

> RAT 2 (ON PERSVID)
> I catched her first!

> RAT 1 (ON PERSVID)
> Fart-face!

> RAT 2 (ON PERSVID)
> Talkin' ta yerself?

Suddenly, RAT 1 explodes in a cloud of green confetti.

> RAT 2 (ON PERSVID)
> Does dis mean I gets to eat him?

The confetti settles to reveal LIZZARDO, a huge gun trained on the second RAT.

> RAT 2 (ON PERSVID)
> Ooopsies.

RAT 2 turns to go... and bumps into LIZZARDO. LIZZARDO swings the gun like a baseball bat, and the RAT sails over the horizon.

The FEMALE has rolled herself into a ball. LIZZARDO picks her up by the scruff and shakes her. She unrolls.

> LIZZARDO (ON PERSVID)
> Mutant, what did I tell ya? Don't leave home without me.

FINN snaps the persvid off.

> FINN
> Don't leave home without me, Mutant.

FINN begins to cry. She looks up at the posters and models.

She leaps up and rips down the posters in a fury of grief. (The "Lizzardo" poster remains.) She smashes the models.

She sweeps the unfinished model off the shelf, and the Lizzardo action figure falls to the floor. As she's about to step on the model, she sees the figure.

She picks up the figure and stares at it. She huddles on the edge of the bed, her knees pulled up to her chin, clutching the Lizzardo figure.

> FINN
> Lights off.

The lights go off, leaving only the city lights shining through the window.

INT. COURTROOM - DAY
FINN, soberly dressed, stands facing the JUDGE, a middle-aged woman. Sitting near FINN is her father, who looks as if he ate something sour and won't admit it. NICKY's parents sit a few rows further back.

                    JUDGE
          Finn, your inexperience and good character incline
          me toward leniency. Your airbike license is revoked.
          You will not be eligible for another until your
          eighteenth birthday. Your vehicle will be placed
          under electronic seal.

FINN closes her eyes and nods.

                    JUDGE
          For the next six months, you may not leave home
          between eight p.m. and seven a.m. unless
          accompanied by a parent. You will also meet with a
          counsellor once a week. Do you have any questions?

                    FINN
          No, Your Honor.

INT. FUNERAL HOME - DAY
NICKY's memorial service is attended by CLASSMATES, TEACHERS, FAMILY FRIENDS. There's no casket; he has been cremated. A MINISTER performs the service at the front of the room.

FINN sits in the back row. No one sits near her. She holds flowers to add to the offerings at the front of the room.

Two GIRLS HER AGE turn to look at her, then turn back and whisper to each other.

MINISTER
...we take comfort in the certainty that Nicky Dicks is
free of trouble, of confusion, of all the sorrow he
knew here on Earth.

FINN
(whispering)
Mutant, did this guy ever meet you?

Quiet, solemn music starts. The minister steps down from the
pulpit. People rise and mill around, talking.

FINN makes her way forward with her flowers. Most people
ignore her. Some scowl, or talk about her behind their hands.

FINN reaches to put her flowers with the others. The two girls
who looked at her earlier bump into her hard. The flowers fall
to the floor.

One girl steps on the flowers. Both smirk at her.

FINN
If Nicky were here, he'd clobber you.

GIRL
But he's not. Whose fault is that?

FINN turns and walks toward the door, her back straight.

EXT. NEW YORK STREET - DAY
FINN makes her way through the crowded streets on foot after
the service. She has been crying.

As she approaches a doorway, one of the RAKASHAS from
the "Roswell-'53" game steps out. FINN gasps.

It wraps its long tongue around a vehicle parked at the curb, and slurps it up–it eats it!

The RAKASHAS disappears into the crowd. Where the vehicle was is a hole in reality, a piece of the twisting multi-color emptiness of hyperspace.

FINN rubs her eyes. When she opens them again, everything is as it was, except the vehicle is missing.

Frightened, she runs for the stairs to a commuter stop.

INT. FINN'S BEDROOM - NIGHT
FINN watches the persvid news, hunched on her bed. She has several channels on, each in its own window on the screen. All the newscasts are winding down.

One channel shows a WEATHERMAN and his weather map.

WEATHERMAN (ON PERSVID)
It's bad news for White Christmas fans–

FINN
Come on, someone must've seen that thing!

WEATHERMAN (ON PERSVID)
That high pressure system down the coast–

On screen, a long RAKASHA's tongue shoots out from off-camera and consumes the WEATHERMAN. A RAKASHA takes his place.

RAKASHA (ON PERSVID)
–will give us clear skies and warmer temperatures.

FINN
No!

94

FINN snaps the persvid off. She runs to the window and looks out. The city is as quiet as it ever is.

                    FINN
          What's going on?

INT. JUVENILE COURT OFFICE - DAY
FINN approaches the RECEPTIONIST at the desk.

                    FINN
          I have an appointment to see a counsellor.

The receptionist consults her computer display.

                    RECEPTIONIST
          You're Finn? Through that door.

The receptionist points to a door.

INT. DR. WYE'S OFFICE - DAY
FINN sticks her head rather timidly into the office. The walls are covered with posters of bands, vid shows and sports and pop culture heroes. There are half-a-dozen wind-up toys and two plastic ray guns on the desk.

DR. WYE sits behind the desk, studying his display screen. He's about 30, handsome and sympathetic.

                    FINN
          Doctor Wye?

He looks up, smiles, rises from the desk chair.

                    DR. WYE
          You must be Finn. Come in, sit down!

FINN smiles, tentatively. She sits on the edge of a big, round chair. (As she talks to WYE, she'll relax, sit further back, maybe pull her feet up.)

> DR. WYE
> I'll bet it's been pretty hard for you, since the accident.

Tears spring to FINN's eyes

> FINN
> Don't be too nice, or I'll cry.

WYE moves to an upholstered chair across from her.

> DR. WYE
> You can cry here. Now, tell me your troubles.

> FINN
> I thought you'd want to talk about the accident.

> DR. WYE
> We can do that later, if you want.

> FINN
> My friends... Since Nicky died, nobody will speak to me. My dad will hardly speak to me. So there's nobody I can ask–

> DR. WYE
> What do you want to ask?

> FINN
> It's... There are these things I see. I don't know if anyone else does.

DR. WYE
Things about your friends or your family?

FINN
No! I mean Things! I saw one on the street, and it ate a car!

DR. WYE
Oh. That kind of things. What are they like?

FINN
They're big, and metal-plated, and they have long tongues.

DR. WYE
When did you see one eat a car?

FINN
On my way home from Nicky's funeral.

DR. WYE
Have you seen it since then?

FINN
Yes, but I can't really have seen it, can I? Someone would have noticed.

DR. WYE
Why is that?

FINN
It ate the weather guy on channel 60 in the middle of the forecast.

DR. WYE
Finn, do you blame yourself for what happened to your friend?

                              FINN
          It was an accident. I did everything I could. The
          witnesses...

                              DR. WYE
          Sometimes what we feel doesn't have much to do
          with what we know. Do you blame yourself?

                              FINN
          I... don't know.

                              DR. WYE
          I think you do, but you don't know it. I think that's
          why you see these creatures.

FINN frowns, trying to understand.

                              DR. WYE
          You feel as if there's a bad person hiding inside you.
          These creatures are your vision of this bad person,
          destroying your world and your happiness.

                              FINN
          But I saw them before Nicky died!

                              DR. WYE
          Where was this?

                              FINN
          In a game, but–

                              DR. WYE
          That must be where your subconscious mind got
          them. In the game, were they frightening?

                              FINN
Yes. But they weren't supposed to be in the game.
It's...
                    (trailing off)
I guess I knew they weren't real. They couldn't be.
But that means I'm crazy.

                            DR. WYE
It means you're upset, and you need help getting over
it. But you can get over it.

WYE unlocks a desk drawer and takes out a vial of little red
pills.

                              FINN
What are those?

                            DR. WYE
Antidepressants.

                              FINN
My best friend just died. Shouldn't I be depressed?

                            DR. WYE
These will make your grief easier to deal with. Take
these, and come back next week. We'll make your
"things" go away.

He holds out the pill bottle. FINN takes it. Its friendly, cartoony label reads, "Mr. Pill! The children's pharmaceutical
specialist."

WYE smiles, warm, sympathetic and handsome.

                              FINN
Thanks. I–I'll see you later, I guess.

EXT. FINN'S BEDROOM - NIGHT
FINN, on her bed, stares at the pill bottle in her hand.

                    FINN
              (rattling the pills)
          They looked a lot friendlier in the same room with
          Doctor Gorgeous.

Frowning, undecided, she turns on the persvid. She channel-surfs by displaying many channels at once, each in its own small window.

One channel shows a "Lizzardo" episode. She enlarges it until it crowds out all but a few of the other channels.

                    FINN
          Princess of Dino-City. I remember this one.

EXT. POST-HOLOCAUST DESERT (ON FINN'S PERS-VID)
On the screen, a cartoony MONSTER slides down the glassy side of a crater and flings a knife at LIZZARDO.

It whizzes past LIZZARDO's ear... and embeds itself in the throat of a RAT NINJA behind him.

LIZZARDO drops flat and trains his enormous gun on the MONSTER.

                    LIZZARDO
          You're either a great shot or a lousy one.

                    MONSTER
          Der best! Vhy do dey vant to kill–look out!

Three more RAT NINJAS leap into the crater. LIZZARDO and the MONSTER fight them.

INT. FINN'S BEDROOM - NIGHT
FINN notices that another channel on the display shows two
RAKASHAS, dancing a pas de deux.

FINN grabs the vial and shakes two pills into her palm.

>   LIZZARDO (ON THE PERSVID)
>   Finn! Put those down!

FINN looks up. The action in the cartoon has stopped, except
for LIZZARDO staring out of the display at her.

>   FINN
>   This is vapor. This is not happening.

>   LIZZARDO
>   (pointing at the pills)
>   I wouldn't take that stuff if I were you.

>   FINN
>   Why? Because it'll make you go away? I hope so.

>   LIZZARDO
>   They hope so, too.

>   FINN
>   You're crazy. Well, I'm crazy, and I'm imagining
>   you, so we're both crazy.

FINN looks at the pills in her hand, then back at LIZZARDO.
She puts the cap on the vial, but doesn't put it down.

>   FINN
>   (warily)
>   Who are "they"?

LIZZARDO

The ones who want to control your head. They want
you to quit seeing things like me. It's messing up the
illusion.

FINN

Actually, what you and your creepy alien pals are
messing up is my life.

LIZZARDO

That's just it. This isn't your life.

FINN

What?

LIZZARDO

Some of it was your life, maybe, when you were a
kid. But you're an adult. You're a Nightspeeder on a–

FINN

I'm a what?

LIZZARDO

A Nightspeeder, a pilot on a hyperspace ship–

FINN

We just found out about hyperspace. There haven't
been any manned flights.

LIZZARDO

Will you shut up and let me finish? You're a
Nightspeeder on a hyperspace ship full of colonists
bound for Deneb Three.

FINN

That's vapor! You stole that from that book,
Nightspeeder, that–

FINN stops, confused.

> LIZZARDO
> ...that you read when you thought you were a reporter in the game. I put it in there. It was supposed to tip you off.

> FINN
> "Roswell-'53" is a game! It's not real!

> LIZZARDO
> Neither is this.

> FINN
> So what're you supposed to be? What do you care?

> LIZZARDO
> I'm your navigator.

FINN laughs at that.

> FINN
> The secret to hyperspace travel is to have cartoons navigate?

> LIZZARDO
> I'm an artificial intelligence. This Lizzardo interface was some big thing from your childhood.

> FINN
> This is my childhood.

> LIZZARDO
> This is an hyperfugue! You've got to snap out of it, Finn.

                         FINN
Yeah, well, I don't think these pills are effective
against "hyperfugues."

                       LIZZARDO
You don't know what I'm talking about.

                         FINN
I don't even know what I'm talking to.

                       LIZZARDO
Look–to travel through hyperspace, you shape it with
your mind. But when you go on a fugue, you lose
control of it.

                         FINN
What's that supposed to mean?

                       LIZZARDO
You're creating fake realities and escaping into them.
First the "Roswell-'53" story, and now this.

INT. *BRAZILIA* COCKPIT
For an instant so brief it's almost subliminal, FINN's her adult
self in the *Brazilia* cockpit, eyeing LIZZARDO.

INT. FINN'S BEDROOM - NIGHT
Immediately, she's the teenager in her bedroom again.

                         FINN
       Stop that!

                       LIZZARDO
       What happened?

FINN

Why would I escape to this? Nicky's dead, nobody'll talk to me, my father hates me, and aliens are eating everything! Do you think I'm having fun?

LIZZARDO

It beats what's really going on.

FINN

Great. What's that?

LIZZARDO

A storm took out our guidance beacon, and we're lost in hyperspace. Four thousand colonists in sleep tanks are counting on you to get us out. And we're under attack by these alien anteater things.

FINN

I thought you said they weren't real!

LIZZARDO

I think you're not supposed to see them. Maybe the pills are supposed to seal up the cracks in this reality you made.

FINN
(depressed)
I think the cracks are in me. This is crazier than seeing aliens who eat cars.

LIZZARDO

Finn, you damned boneheaded human, fight back!

FINN

Against what? How? Maybe Dr. Wye is right–maybe I should take the pills!

Furious, FINN shakes out half-a-dozen pills and raises them toward her mouth.

> LIZZARDO
> You've got passengers counting on you! You're supposed to take care of them!

INT. *BRAZILIA* COCKPIT
Again, FINN and LIZZARDO are suddenly the adult FINN and LIZZARDO in the cockpit of the *Brazilia*.

INT. FINN'S BEDROOM - NIGHT
FINN drops the pills and covers her face with both hands.

> FINN
> I said I'd take care of him. Of them. Oh, I don't remember!

> LIZZARDO
> (gently)
> Yes, you do.

FINN hears a knock at the front door of the apartment.

INT. FINN'S LIVING ROOM - NIGHT
FINN'S FATHER opens the front door to reveal WYE and two white-clad ORDERLIES.

FINN'S FATHER looks stern and sad and points the way to FINN's room.

INT. FINN'S BEDROOM - NIGHT
WYE enters FINN's bedroom. The persvid is on (LIZZARDO is being chased by a horde of RATS). The pills are scattered on the bed. There's no one in the room.

One of the ORDERLIES goes to the open window and looks out.

                    ORDERLY
        Sir!

WYE looks out and sees the fire escape.

                    DR. WYE
        Go down this way. We'll take the stairs.

One ORDERLY climbs out the window as WYE and the OTHER head for the bedroom door.

                    LIZZARDO (ON THE PERSVID)
        You street lizards couldn't catch Lyme disease at a
        tick convention!

EXT. FINN'S APARTMENT BUILDING GARAGE - NIGHT
FINN pries the electronic seal off the ignition of her impounded bike. The seal's alarm goes off as it falls.

FINN leaps onto the bike and starts it up, as the ORDERLY drops down from the fire escape.

                    ORDERLY
        Hey–stop! Stop!

FINN drives straight at him. He throws himself flat as she climbs steeply and disappears into the night.

EXT. NEW YORK STREETS & SKIES - NIGHT
FINN zooms through the canyons of the New York streets. It's very late, but the city's still awake and busy. Lights flash, ads scroll, and the atmosvids are running.

FINN tears past an ad for the LIZZARDO show.

                    FINN
          Any more advice, Hallucination Boy?

LIZZARDO springs out of the ad, somersaults and lands on an
invisible surface next to FINN.

                  LIZZARDO
          Since you ask, yeah.

                    FINN
          No! No more crap about Nightspeeders and
          hyperspace and hyperfugues!

                  LIZZARDO
          Then why didn't you stick around and let the good
          Doctor Wye take you away?

                    FINN
          I'm afraid, Lizzardo. I'm afraid of you, and him,
          and... I'm afraid of me, too.

                  LIZZARDO
          They're playing with you. The more you stretch this
          out, the happier they are.

                    FINN
          Who are "they"?

                  LIZZARDO
          Maybe your metal anteater aliens. They seem to be
          living in hyperspace.

                    FINN
          I'm supposed to believe that? You're a figment of my
          imagination! Go away!

                     108

LIZZARDO
What're you doing?

FINN
Trying to find a place to hide.

FINN gazes out over the city in dawning horror.

FINN
Oh, no. No!

The city is being eaten by thousands of RAKASHAS. The
Empire State Building is being unmade from the bottom up,
and the space filled with churning colors. The Chrysler
Building has holes chewed through it, showing patches of hyperspace.

LIZZARDO
They're feeding on your reality. You create it, and
they consume it. You've got to stop this, before they
really do drive you crazy!

FINN
I don't know how!

<u>EXT. STATUE OF LIBERTY - NIGHT</u>
As FINN reaches the Statue of Liberty, a black hovership, like
a helicopter without rotors, drops out of the sky. A dozen
smaller flyers rise toward her from a harbor island.

FINN sees WYE through the hovership windshield, a micro-
phone in his hand. Two ORDERLIES stand behind him.

DR. WYE (AMPLIFIED)
Finn! Please, land your bike and come back with me.
We'll make this go away–

FINN's view of the scene flickers from WYE and his OR-
DERLIES in the hovership, to YARROW and his M.I.B.s in a
black sedan... and finally to YAMA himself, a huge, human-
shaped battle suit with a skull in the helmet, and two RAKA-
SHAS. They revert to WYE and his ORDERLIES.

                    DR. WYE (AMPLIFIED)
          Don't you want that, Finn?

                    LIZZARDO
          Finn, you can make this go away. You have to
          destroy this fake reality.

                    FINN
                  (laughs bitterly)
          Then where will I live?

                    LIZZARDO
          You made this! Concentrate, and you can pop this
          sucker like a balloon!

                    FINN
          What if I go with him?

                    LIZZARDO
          He'll play with your head until he uses you up. He's
          one of them!

                    FINN
          One of the aliens?

                    LIZZARDO
          I can't tell when you keep changing him around like
          that.

                    FINN
          I'm not changing him!

LIZZARDO

You're a Nightspeeder! You're making this reality!
But you're letting him run it!

DR. WYE (AMPLIFIED)

Finn, if you don't land, the police will arrest you. I
can't help you then.

The smaller vehicles, closer now, have police markings.

LIZZARDO

The colonists are counting on you. Come on, partner,
blow it all up!

FINN

I DON'T KNOW HOW!

The police vehicles close on FINN. As they do, they become a
swarm of RAKASHAS, then turn back to police flyers.

FINN looks up. The Moon is being eaten by the RAKASHAS.
The stars are winking out.

In determination and despair, FINN rises on the foot pegs of
her bike. She lifts her arms and clenches her fists.

DR. WYE (AMPLIFIED)

Finn, don't do this–

FINN's eyes squeeze shut. Her expression is fierce. The air
crackles around her. Turbulence buffets the police vehicles.

LIZZARDO

Do it! Now!

INT. *BRAZILIA* COCKPIT
Flash: The adult FINN throws her head back. Her face wears the same fierce expression as her younger self.

EXT. STATUE OF LIBERTY - NIGHT
FINN flings her arms wide, as if throwing something. Her body glows with energy. She SCREAMS, wordless and angry.

> DR. WYE
> No! No!

A blast with FINN at its center rips outward, consuming everything in blinding light and terrible noise...

> MORPH TO:

INT. *BRAZILIA* COCKPIT
FINN's aboard her ship. The controls are wild with flashing lights and alarms. The monitors show the hyperspace storm.

> FINN
> I'm back in Kansas.

> LIZZARDO
> Yeah, kid, but they're still going to kill your dog.
> We're under attack!

EXT. *BRAZILIA* - IN HYPERSPACE
The ship is caught in the hyperstorm and under attack from the RAKASHAS, who are literally eating the hull.

INT. *BRAZILIA* COCKPIT
The viewscreen shows the RAKASHAS' assault.

> FINN
> Are they–Are they from my mind?

LIZZARDO
You're not imagining them. The med sensors would
reveal that, I think.

FINN
The passengers?

LIZZARDO
All stable.

FINN
Let's see if we can ditch these cooties.

FINN reaches into the control panel lights.

EXT. *BRAZILIA* - IN HYPERSPACE
The ship surges forward. The RAKASHAS fall from the
ship's side, leaving deep pits in the hull.

INT. *BRAZILIA* COCKPIT
LIZZARDO
No ship's ever experienced anything like this. Except
maybe the *Cairo*.

FINN gives him an alarmed look and returns to the controls.

FINN
Where's the beacon, damn it!

LIZZARDO
If you could impose some order for about a minute, I
might get a fix.

FINN appears to meditate, with difficulty.

EXT. *BRAZILIA* - IN HYPERSPACE

A pocket of calm forms around the ship, less like the tunnel that FINN had created earlier and more like a cavern.

> FINN
>
> I don't know how long I can hold this. Where's the beacon?

> LIZZARDO
>
> A little more–There!

The once bright yellow beacon is a distorted, pale ribbon of light, broken as though coming through in pulses.

INT. *BRAZILIA* COCKPIT

FINN and LIZZARDO exchange looks of triumph.

> LIZZARDO
>
> Beacon signal at thirty-three percent.

On screen, a second beam of light appears, coming from a different direction. A third appears from another direction. More beacons appear, like the work of an insane weaver.

> FINN
>
> What's going on?

> LIZZARDO
>
> They're all the Deneb beacon! The storm's reflecting it, breaking it up.

> FINN
>
> Which one should we follow?

> LIZZARDO
>
> I can't tell!

RAKASHAS launch themselves from the chaos toward the ship.

                    LIZZARDO
          Our friends are back.

The pocket of calm shrivels as the RAKASHAS approach.

                    FINN
                (to monitor)
          This is Nightspeeder Finn of the *Brazilia*. We come
          in peace! We don't know what you intend, but you're
          hurting our ship!

                    LIZZARDO
          Hull integrity breached.

                    FINN
          The passengers! My God–

                    LIZZARDO
          Emergency systems will preserve them, if those
          things don't get into the hold.

                    FINN
          What's going to stop them?

                    LIZZARDO
          When you made that pocket in the storm, it slowed
          them down.

                    FINN
          I couldn't do it for long.

                    LIZZARDO
          If you could create a new reality here–

                    FINN
        I don't want a new reality, I want armor plating!

FINN concentrates. A barrier of seamless steel forms around
the ship.

The RAKASHAS fall back from the barrier. Then they surge
forward again, eating the steel plating.

                  LIZZARDO
        That's slowing them.

                    FINN
        So as long as I can make things up, we can hold them
        off?

                  LIZZARDO
        Unless they die of over-eating, we'll still be trapped
        here. And you'll have to sleep sometime.

                    FINN
        Do you have an imagination?

                  LIZZARDO
        Nightspeeders have imaginations. Navigators have
        brains.

                    FINN
        To hell with it. Let's go on the offensive.

EXT. *BRAZILIA* - IN HYPERSPACE
The ship turns and rams a horde of RAKASHAS, then races
on.

More RAKASHAS launch themselves toward the ship. In
spite of FINN's piloting, the *Brazilia* sustains more damage.

The ship lurches sideways, as though caught by gravity.

INT. *BRAZILIA* COCKPIT
                    LIZZARDO
          We're being pulled down!

                    FINN
          There's no "down" in hyperspace.

                    LIZZARDO
          There is now.

EXT. *BRAZILIA* - YAMA'S WORLD
Pursued by RAKASHAS, the *Brazilia* drops through strange
clouds. It CRASHES into a hellish dreamscape of gigantic
ruined machines, mountain-sized skeletons of fanged and
clawed buffalo, oily-looking rivers and cracked, burning earth.

INT. *BRAZILIA*
FINN pulls herself off the floor.

                    FINN
          Ouch. That's gravity.

                    LIZZARDO
          There's breathable atmosphere out there.

                    FINN
          In hyperspace? I'm imagining this.

                    LIZZARDO
          Then we're both delusional.

                    FINN
          The passengers?

LIZZARDO
All stable, in emergency mode.

EXT. YAMA'S WORLD
The RAKASHAS regroup on a plain far from the ship. In gravity, they've switched from air force to infantry. From out of their midst comes a new manifestation–the LOCOSTORMER.

INT. *BRAZILIA* COCKPIT
FINN and LIZZARDO stare at the approaching behemoth.

FINN
(doubtfully)
I think this calls for something big.

EXT. *BRAZILIA* - IN YAMA'S WORLD
FINN transforms the *Brazilia* into the THUNDERHORN.

The tide of battle turns as the THUNDERHORN plows through the RAKASHAS, making mincemeat out of them.

LIZZARDO
Yahoo!

After a mighty battle, the LOCOSTORMER wins. The THUNDERHORN reshapes into the damaged *Brazilia*.

RAKASHAS still swarm over the ship. Their long tongues twine around every outcropping, holding it motionless.

INT. *BRAZILIA* COCKPIT
FINN collapses under the strain.

LIZZARDO
Finn?

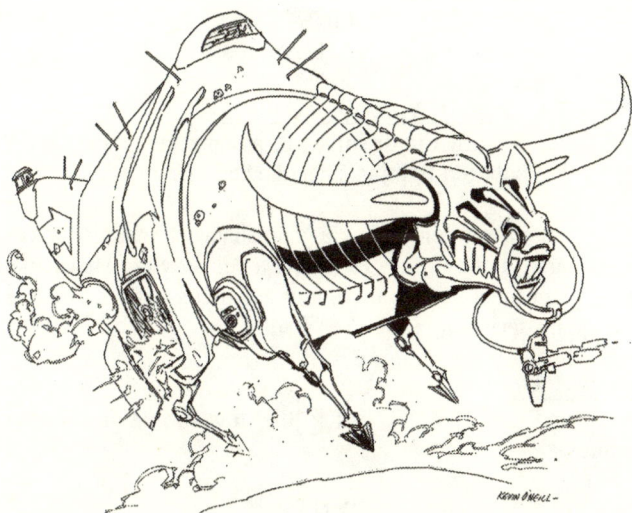

Thunderhorn and Locostormer

FINN
My head–Let me rest, Lizzardo.

EXT. *BRAZILIA* - IN YAMA'S WORLD
The LOCOSTORMER dissolves to assume the shape of the enemy they've been fighting since the beginning–YAMA.

YAMA manifests himself as a man-shaped thing, partly organic, partly battle-armor. He wears a helmet with what looks like a giant metallic spinal column extending from it. Visible through his face plate is a naked skull.

INT. *BRAZILIA*
FINN and LIZZARDO watch the transformation on the monitor.

FINN
Oh, my God.

FINN throws out her hands, concentrating furiously.

EXT. YAMA'S WORLD
Steel walls 30 feet thick and high enough to shield the *Brazilia* rise out of the ground, flinging back the RAKASHAS.

YAMA laughs, a ghastly, ghostly sound.

RAKASHAS surround the high steel walls and wait impassively.

INT. *BRAZILIA*
FINN covers her ears. The laughter grows louder.

EXT. YAMA'S WORLD
YAMA walks straight at the walls, which melt around him. He stops in front of the *Brazilia*.

                    YAMA
        Come out, Finn.

INT. *BRAZILIA*
                    FINN
                (to monitor)
        What do you want?

                    YAMA (ON MONITOR)
        You.

                    FINN
        I have passengers to deliver.

                    YAMA (ON MONITOR)
        You have nothing.

EXT. YAMA'S WORLD
YAMA raises his hand. FINN's steel walls burst into flame
like paper, flaring up and dying within seconds.

A wind blows away the ashes, then picks up strength and tears
away pieces of the *Brazilia*. First the hull, then larger sections
of the ship, scatter across the plain.

INT. *BRAZILIA* COCKPIT
FINN clings to the pilot's couch as the ship rocks. Harsh light
penetrates broken seams in the hull.

EXT. YAMA'S WORLD
The wind strips the *Brazilia* to its skeletal frame, the passengers' capsules and the cockpit.

INT. *BRAZILIA* HOLD
YAMA enters what's left of the hold, and surveys the passengers.

YAMA
Delightful.

FINN leaps down from the cockpit, into the hold.

FINN
Who are you?

YAMA
Nightspeeder Dorje of the *Cairo*. But you may call
me Yama.

YAMA rests his hand on one of the passenger's capsules.

FINN concentrates, and a shimmering field pushes YAMA's
hand away.

YAMA
Don't be annoying.

FINN
They're my passengers. I'm supposed to protect
them.

YAMA
You haven't done a very good job.

LIZZARDO appears, standing between FINN and YAMA.

LIZZARDO
So far, they're all snug in their beds.

FINN
What do you want?

YAMA
What have you got?

LIZZARDO
A pain in the butt that looks like you.

YAMA
Then I'll take my business elsewhere.

EXT. YAMA'S WORLD - MOUNTAIN TOP
YAMA and FINN blink into existence on a mountain top.
Below are the skeletal *Brazilia* and thousands of RAKASHAS
around it.

FINN
Take me back!

YAMA
Soon.

FINN
Restore my link to my ship!

YAMA
I thought it would be nice to talk without distractions.

FINN
Lizzardo isn't a distraction.

YAMA
No, he's a nuisance. Without him, you'd still be a
reporter chasing flying saucers, and I'd be thwarting
you at every turn.

FINN
That's what you want?

YAMA

That was the most fun I've had in... a long time.
Playing with your memories was refreshing. I've
grown tired of mine.

FINN

Why?

YAMA

Why did God give living things free will? Because
Hell is when nothing surprises you.

FINN

Did you make the storm to trap us here?

YAMA

No. The Rakashas–that's what I call the simple-
minded things that attacked you–let me know you
were here, so I came.

FINN

To torture me.

YAMA

You've always liked excitement. Haven't I given you
some?

FINN

Thanks a lot.

YAMA

Don't be bitter, Finn. Here, we are kings of infinite
space.

<u>INT. ARABIAN PALACE</u>
FINN, in the robes of a sultana, reclines in a luxurious room.
A SLAVE offers food and wine. YAMA, every inch a sultan
except for his skull-like face, stands beside her.

                    YAMA
          You can have whatever you want.

                    FINN
          And the price?

                    YAMA
          That you test your skills against mine. Is that so
          horrible?

                    FINN
          I have to get my passengers home.

YAMA's face turns into EDUARDO's.

                    YAMA
          You needn't miss your friends.

                    FINN
          No!

FINN makes a furious gesture.

<u>EXT. YAMA'S WORLD - MOUNTAIN TOP</u>
YAMA and FINN return to the mountain.

                    YAMA
          You didn't like that? You create something, then.

                    FINN
          What happened to you? How did you become... what
          you are?

125

YAMA

A storm, like you. But I was alone. My ship didn't
have A.I. navigation. All I had was war with those
fiends, the Rakashas.

FINN

They attacked you?

YAMA

They're attracted to our thoughts. They come like
locusts. At first, they were shapeless blobs of light,
but as I fought them, they revealed their true selves.

FINN

I thought they served you?

YAMA

I became their master, before I died.

FINN

Excuse me?

YAMA

My ship's life support systems failed after a few
months. But I'd learned much about shaping reality.
My passengers could live forever in suspended
animation. So I absorbed them into myself as I died.

FINN

One thousand passengers... You killed one thousand
passengers–

YAMA

They sleep within me. If they died, I would, too. But
now I'm immortal. You could be the same.

FINN

Not if that's the price.

YAMA

Your ship's too damaged to leave hyperspace. If you wake your passengers, they'll go mad. You might as well use them.

FINN

There must be a way to get them home.

YAMA

Of course there is.

FINN

Tell me.

YAMA

No. You're the first uncertainty in what has become a very dull existence.

FINN

It'll go on being dull if I don't cooperate.

YAMA

That's why I'm making you an offer. We duel on a battlefield of my devising. If I win, you stay, and your passengers keep us both alive. If you win, I send you and your cargo on your way. Fair?

FINN

It would be, if I could trust you.

YAMA

If you could trust me, it'd be much less exciting.

EXT. NEW YORK STREETS - AFTERNOON

The landscape twists, shrugs... and becomes the New York City of FINN's youth. But instead of humans, the inhabitants are RAKASHAS doing human things: waiting for commuter pods, reading newspapers, walking demon dogs, driving air cars.

                         YAMA
         I'll even give you the home turf advantage.

                         FINN
         Can I hear the terms before I applaud?

                         YAMA
         We'll have a race. You on your faithful airbike–tell
         me, did it have a name?

                         FINN
         Yeah. "My bike."

                         YAMA
         We'll follow your old delivery route. Whoever
         completes it first wins all.

                         FINN
         What are you driving?

                         YAMA
         An airbike, a car–since you have familiarity on your
         side, I reserve the right to take a few liberties.

                         FINN
         Nothing that wasn't legal on New York streets in
         2081.

                         YAMA
         Anything else would spoil the fun.

FINN

Let me talk it over with Lizzardo.

YAMA

Certainly. You should have a cheerleader.

LIZZARDO appears in a cartoon puff of smoke. FINN glares at YAMA, who shrugs.

LIZZARDO

Finn! I saw it all on the monitor.

FINN and LIZZARDO step out of hearing of YAMA and his troops.

FINN

Well?

LIZZARDO

I think he really is bored, Finn. Nuts, but bored. He wants to make this last.

FINN

So he'll drag out the game-playing, rather than squashing us like bugs. But he may have miscalculated.

LIZZARDO

You can beat him?

FINN

He must be judging my skills by the way I relived the accident with Nicky. I've improved.

YAMA

Do you accept the terms?

FINN and LIZZARDO return to YAMA. He stands beside an airbike that looks like the one from FINN's youth.

> FINN
> My co-pilot and I are ready to race.

> YAMA
> No room for a co-pilot. You'll be carrying a passenger.

A figure forms out of thin air before them. It resolves into KAZ, the boy FINN met in the Starbridge elevator.

He looks around at the New York streets crammed with RA-KASHAS, his eyes wide with growing fear.

FINN steps forward and puts her hands on his shoulders.

> FINN
> It's OK, Kaz. Remember me, Finn? The Nightspeeder for your ship?

> KAZ
> This isn't Deneb Three.

> FINN
> You're dreaming. You can have some pretty wild dreams in suspended animation.

> KAZ
> What are you doing in my dream?

> FINN
> I said I'd take care of you, didn't I?

YAMA
I'm sure you'll keep your word. A race like this can
be deadly for passengers.

FINN
You can't hurt him.

YAMA
Unless you lose the race. It'd be sad if you hurt him
in order to win.

EXT. NEW YORK STREETS & SKIES (IN YAMA'S
WORLD) - AFTERNOON
FINN sets off on her bike, KAZ behind her. A dark cloud
slides across the Sun. A drizzle of rain begins.

A silver airbike forms under YAMA. He takes off after FINN.

LIZZARDO stands flanked by RAKASHAS. They flick out
their tongues and give him the RAKASHAS equivalent of a
smile. LIZZARDO scowls, shrugs and settles down to wait.

FINN races through the city. The landscape is not always true
to her memories, though there are glimpses of the hospital, the
bookstore.

The weather grows worse. The storm is fiercer than the one in
which NICKY died: Lightning flashes, and winds rock the
bike.

FINN banks around a corner and finds a 20-storey tower of
steaming mechanical rubble–a fragment of YAMA's reality.

Over her shoulder, FINN sees YAMA behind her. He and his
bike transform into a sleek metal monster, arrowing toward
her.

FINN drops two storeys and flies through an archway that opens all the way through a city-block-sized building. YAMA misses the opening. He'll have to go around the building.

FINN has gained almost a block length. Many of the buildings around her are the skeletal, smoking structures of YAMA's World.

>   KAZ
>   If you weren't here, I'd be a little scared.

>   FINN
>   Just hang on tight and do everything I tell you.

FINN tears around another corner ahead of YAMA, who's now a silver biker in a skull-shaped helmet.

Behind YAMA, half-a-dozen New York City police flyers appear. Their drivers, at first COPS, transform into MEN IN BLACK, then RAKASHAS, then back to cops.

Ahead is the intersection where the young FINN narrowly avoided the taxi. Past it, two RAKASHAS link their long tongues together to form the finish line.

Between FINN and the finish line is the building decorated with stainless steel gargoyles, where NICKY was killed.

All around, buildings transform into surrealistically Gothic shapes, things from YAMA's imagination... except for the building where NICKY died, which stays as it was.

FINN looks back at YAMA. His silver skull helmet opens its mouth and laughs. He's gaining.

An air taxi shoots around the corner, heading for FINN's bike. It's so close that she can see the RAKASHAS driving.

FINN dives to pass below the taxi, but it also drops. She pulls the bike's nose up and climbs like a rocket.

She keeps climbing–he's going to fly above the gargoyles! It looks like she's going to make it...

A "Roswell-'53"-style U.F.O. plunges from the roiling clouds at her. YAMA is fixing the race. He won't let her win.

                    FINN
          You bastard!

FINN can't turn fast enough to avoid the gargoyle that killed NICKY. They're going to hit it.

FINN twists in the saddle and pushes KAZ down flat.

The gargoyle's beak slams hard into FINN's back, then strikes the back of her head as she collapses over KAZ.

The bike slips sideways and begins to fall. KAZ SCREAMS.

FINN is bloody and gasping for air. With the last of her strength, she wrenches the bike out of its dive.

YAMA is almost on her. She cranks the throttle and plunges through the outstretched tongues of the two RAKASHAS marking the finish line. Their tongues snap back like rubber bands.

FINN lands the bike with an ungainly thump.

                    KAZ
          We win! Nightspeeders are best!

FINN's face is crumpled with pain. She slides off the bike and lands hard on the pavement.

KAZ
Nightspeeder? Nightspeeder!

FINN's face goes slack.

EXT. YAMA'S WORLD
The city streets, airbike, all the simulations of New York melt away, leaving the landscape of YAMA-controlled hyperspace.

The image of KAZ fades away.

FINN lies on the barren ground, eyes closed, hands crossed on her chest. The RAKASHA hordes surround her, though at a distance.

LIZZARDO vaults over the RAKASHAS to get to FINN's side.

LIZZARDO
Finn! You can't be dead!

YAMA
Look around. This is my kingdom. Nothing of hers is left here. What do your med-sensors tell you?

LIZZARDO
That she's dead.

FINN's body is slowly absorbed into the ground beneath her and the air around her. LIZZARDO scrabbles his hands over the ground where she was, as if hoping to feel what he can't see.

LIZZARDO
She won! You can't kill her!

YAMA

She died. Her passengers are mine. And, so, I
suppose, are you.

LIZZARDO stares in horror at YAMA.

A figure pushes through the ring of RAKASHAS–a human-
sized shadow. It passes the exulting YAMA and leans over
LIZZARDO.

LIZZARDO looks up. The shadow becomes a barely-visible
ghost figure, then grows more solid. It's NICKY, as he was
before the accident in FINN's youth. He smiles at LIZ-
ZARDO.

NICKY

Wait for it.

YAMA

Who are you?

The sky writhes and becomes FINN's face, looking down.

FINN

Now, it's my turn.

LIZZARDO

FINN?

YAMA's reality melts away into a landscape of trees, mead-
ows and streams. The *Brazilia*'s ruins lie in an open field.

The ground rises around YAMA. It becomes a giant stone
hand that closes around him, imprisoning him.

FINN blows gently on the crowd of panicky RAKASHAS.
They shrink and change shape, to become the cartoon RATS.

The RATS stare at and poke one another, laugh hysterically and begin to investigate their new environment. More RATS tumble off the skeletal frame of the *Brazilia*.

FINN returns to her normal shape and size.

> FINN
>
> Nicky?

> NICKY
>
> Just his memory. You've been carrying me a long time.

> FINN
>
> Do you forgive me?

> NICKY
>
> I can't, stupid, I'm dead. You have to forgive yourself. Do you?

> FINN
>
> I guess I did.

NICKY melts away.

YAMA, angry and frightened, struggles in the stone hand's grip.

> YAMA
>
> You can't get rid of me! I'm part of hyperspace! I'm immortal!

> FINN
>
> Because the passengers from your ship keep you alive. You said that.

Another stone hand forms beside the first, takes the metallic "spinal column" of YAMA's helmet between thumb and forefinger.

                              FINN
              Is this the link to them?

                              YAMA
        No!

The stone hand snaps the metal cord off at YAMA's helmet.

YAMA's demon-form shrinks into the man he was, the Hindu Nightspeeder of the *Cairo*. Sorrow and fear mingle on his face. Then his body collapses, decays to a skeleton, turns to eddying dust.

The stone hands sink back into the ground.

The blowing dust from YAMA's form whirls about and becomes an early hyperspace ship, the *Cairo*.

                            LIZZARDO
              The *Cairo*?

                              FINN
              Complete with passengers. This has been a long
              nightmare for them.

                            LIZZARDO
        What about us?

FINN grins, raises her arms like a magician conjuring a huge illusion.

The *Brazilia* reshapes itself, growing like an organic thing. FINN snaps her fingers...

                               137

INT. *BRAZILIA* COCKPIT
...and FINN and LIZZARDO are back in the cockpit. The viewscreen shows the swirling colors of hyperspace.

> LIZZARDO
> Very nice. Where's the beacon?

> FINN
> If you have the right kind of shoes, you just click the heels together...

> LIZZARDO
> I'm a rational, scientific A.I. If you're going to do magic, I wash my holographic hands of you.

> FINN
> Lighten up, partner. Click, click.

EXT. *BRAZILIA* - IN HYPERSPACE
A dark spot appears in the chaos. It widens, opening onto the star-spangled darkness of normal space. A green-and-white planet lies at its center–Deneb Three.

INT. *BRAZILIA* COCKPIT
> FINN
> Who needs a beacon? I'm part of hyperspace now. I can enter and leave it at any place I choose.

> LIZZARDO
> Why didn't Yama?

> FINN
> He would've died if he'd left. He learned the secret too late. He was a prisoner here, not a god.

INT. DENEB THREE - SPACE STATION

JEN, a female technician, works at a wall of electronics. HASSAN, flight controller for the Deneb Three station, sits at a control panel. He looks from it to the viewscreen.

> HASSAN
> The *Brazilia*'s late.

The viewscreen shows a circle of robots in space connected by beams of light. The gate's open between them. The beacon streams from the station into the gate, and disappears.

> JEN
> How long till we have to close the gate?

> HASSAN
> Five minutes.

On screen, a patch of space near the gate lightens, seems to bulge inward and swirl like water draining.

HASSAN slaps the controls in front of him, and ALARMS sound.

> HASSAN
> Emergency condition! All traffic, clear the gate quadrant!

> JEN
> Holy Mother, what is that thing?

"That thing" resolves into a second gate, sharp-edged and stable. The *Brazilia* soars out of it into real space.

> HASSAN
> Oh. My. God.

FINN (V.O.)
Deneb, this is *Brazilia* requesting docking berth. Did
I keep you waiting?

HASSAN
(dazed)
Just a little. Welcome to Deneb Three, *Brazilia*.

The *Cairo* follows the *Brazilia* out of the new gate.

HASSAN
Brazilia, hold position! Incoming ship, identify
yourself!

FINN's image comes up on the viewscreen, showing her head
and shoulders backed by the cockpit of the *Brazilia*.

FINN
It's the *Cairo*, six years late. The passengers are safe.

HASSAN
What about the pilot?

FINN
Dead. He died... fighting for his ship.

INT. *BRAZILIA* COCKPIT
LIZZARDO sits on the edge of the control panel, kicking his
heels. The space station looms on the viewscreen.

LIZZARDO
What are you going to say when he asks where that
gate came from?

FINN
I'll tell him. I'm going to tell anyone who wants to
know.

LIZZARDO
You want to hold a press conference?

FINN
Lizzardo, I think I can teach people how to do this.

LIZZARDO
To open gates?

FINN
From anywhere, to anywhere! Yes!

LIZZARDO
Well, you won't need an A.I. navigator anymore.

FINN
Why not?

LIZZARDO
You're the new queen of hyperspace. How lost can you get?

FINN
There's more than one kind of "lost," partner. Your resignation is not accepted.

LIZZARDO
Where are we going?

FINN
Want to go see if there's life in the Horse Nebula?...

A pause. FINN looks at the rose in the bulb on the wall. She touches it, then brings it to her nose and inhales.

FINN (cont'd)
...But I have a stop to make on the way

EXT. BRAZILIA
END CREDITS start as the ship approaches Deneb Three and
we

FADE OUT.

THE END

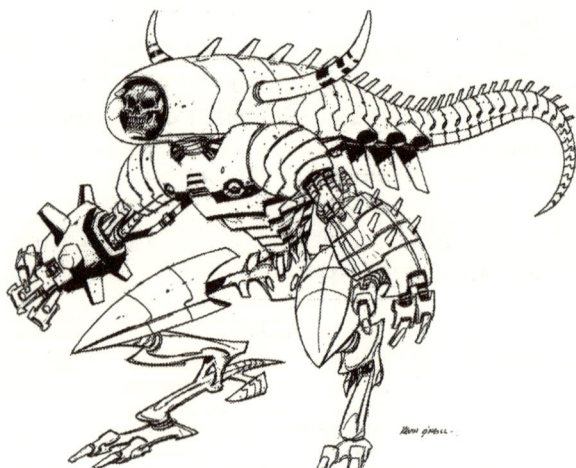

Yama

ABOUT THE AUTHORS

Writers **Emma BULL** and **Will SHETTERLY** have written novels, short stories, screenplays, comic books, poetry and essays. Emma was a finalist for the Hugo, Nebula and World Fantasy Award for *Bone Dance*. She is also a singer, guitarist, and songwriter; her duo, the *Flash Girls*, won the Minnesota Music Award for World Folk Music. Will won the Minnesota Book Award for *Elsewhere*. He is proudest of *Dogland*, a novel inspired by his childhood on a tourist attraction in Florida. He ran for Governor of Minnesota and finished third in a field of six. Will and Emma live in Bisbee, Arizona, their favorite small town in the U.S.

Illustrator **Kevin O'NEILL** is one of the most distinctive artists having come out of England in the last decade. His peculiar, angular look and twisted imagination have enlightened the pages of many comic-book series, such as *ABC Warriors*, *Nemesis* and *Batman*. He is also the artist of the critically-acclaimed graphic novel *Metalzoic* and the co-creator (with Pat Mills) of the cult character, *Marshal Law*. Kevin is currently working with Alan Moore on *The League of Extraordinary Gentlemen*.

www.ingramcontent.com/pod-product-compliance
Lightning Source LLC
Chambersburg PA
CBHW031852090426
42741CB00005B/461